MOHAMMED, BUDDHA, AND CHRIST

MOHAMMED, BUDDHA, AND CHRIST

FOUR LECTURES

ON

NATURAL AND REVEALED RELIGION.

BY

MARCUS DODS, D. D.

GYAN

Published by

GYAN

Gyan Publishing House
5, Ansari Road
Daryaganj, New Delhi-110002
Phone: 011-47034999, 9811692060
E-mail: books@gyanbooks.com

Distribution Network
gyanbooks.com
India, USA, Canada, UK, Australia, France

ISBN : 978-81-212-2107-8 (HB)
First Published, 1877

2nd Impression 2021

Printed at: Gyan Press, Delhi.

Mohammed, Buddha, and Christ
Author: Marcus Dods

MOHAMMED, BUDDHA, AND CHRIST.

FOUR LECTURES

ON

NATURAL AND REVEALED RELIGION.

BY

MARCUS DODS, D.D.

London:

HODDER AND STOUGHTON,

27, PATERNOSTER ROW.

MDCCCLXXVII.

CONTENTS.

LECTURE I.

MOHAMMEDANISM.

LECTURE II.

MOHAMMEDANISM.

LECTURE IV.

THE PERFECT RELIGION.

I.

MOHAMMEDANISM:

ITS CREED AND PRACTICE.

"*Say: He is one God:*
God the Everlasting:
He begetteth not, and He is not begotten;
And there is none like unto Him."

KORAN, Sura cxii.

I.

FIFTEEN per cent. of our fellow-men are understood to be Mohammedans, and from forty to fifty millions of these are fellow-subjects of our own, whose faith may any day materially affect our most important interests, yet I cannot take for granted that you have already in your minds any clear conception of the religion of Islam. One of the best modern authorities on the subject remarks[1] that, although Islam has been described in so many books, even educated people know little more about it than that the Turks are polygamists. If this is extreme, it must yet be owned that the knowledge of this great religion which most people are content with is confined to the fact that it originated with Mohammed, and makes its devotees polygamous and fatalistic persecutors, who abstain from wine. Happily the creed of Islam is brief

[1] Sprenger's *Das Leben und die Lehre des Moh.* ii. 181.

and easily learned; its worship, though somewhat formal, is as simple as Calvin or Knox could have wished; and the conduct it enjoins, if not always the purest and loftiest, is always perfectly intelligible and practicable.

The articles of the Mohammedan creed are six. Every Moslem must believe in the unity of God, in the Angels, the Koran, the Prophets, the Day of Judgment, and the Decrees of God. Or, as the Koran itself puts it, "Whosoever believeth not on God, and His Angels, and His Books, and His Apostles, and on the Last Day, he verily hath erred with far gone error."[1] But the brief confession which—uttered with upheld forefinger to denote the unity of God—makes any man a Mohammedan, is the world-renowned formula, "There is no God but God, and Mohammed is the Prophet of God." All that is essential and peculiar to this religion, its whole strength and weakness, is embraced in this twofold assertion.

Mohammed was much more of a poet than of a thinker. He had no capacity for profound theological inquiry, but his natural penetration and sense repudiated idolatry as monstrous, while his intensely religious temperament made God more necessary to him than food or drink. His idea of God was originally formed in pre-

[1] Sura iv. 135.

sence of, and in opposition to, idolatry, and not with any definite knowledge of, or reference to, Christianity. Turning with distaste from the discussions of tritheistic and Arian Christians, he asserted the existence and supremacy of one God in a form level to the capacity of his hearers, and in the definite and absolute terms of a mind untrammelled and undisturbed by the suggestions of a better instructed theology.[1] "Surely now are they infidels who say God is a third of three, for there is no God but one God. . . The Messiah, son of Mary, is but an apostle; other apostles have flourished before him; and his mother was a just person; they both ate food."[2] The extent of his inquiries into the doctrine of the Trinity, which he thus denounces, may be gathered from the fact that he believed the Virgin Mary (whom he also confounded with Miriam, the sister of Moses[3]) to be the third person worshipped by Trinitarians, as the Mother of God, with the Father and the Son.[4]

But the Unitarianism of Mohammed, however ill-instructed, had the initial advantage of

[1] Cf. Voltaire, *Essai sur les mœurs*, c. vi.

[2] Sura v. 77.

[3] All that can be said in explanation of this anachronism will be found in Reland's *De Rel. Moh.* p. 211, and Rodwell's *Koran*, p. 422.

[4] Sura v. 116, and especially vi. 101.

an easy and forcible presentation. There is one God, and through me, Mohammed, that God summons you to submit to Him. This was the simple gospel which gave birth to the most aggressive religion the world has ever known. Submission, says Bishop Butler, is the whole of religion. This was what Mohammed laid hold of, and Islam, that is, Submission, was the religion he proclaimed. Let all things come into the harmony of obedience to one God. It is a great awakening to a man when he learns that the universe is one, that one government, one system, one idea, one Will orders the whole. Certainly it was the time of Arabia's regeneration, as it was one of the grand moments of the world's history, when Mohammed, in the strength of his new faith and triumphing over all his native superstitions and the associations of his childhood, entered the temple of Mecca, and shivered the three hundred and sixty idols with the cry, The truth has come, let falsehood disappear. Round this belief, that one only was supreme, and that He had a will to execute on earth through all who believed in Him, the dislocated tribes of Arabia united; this for the time became the compact centre of the earth; and all who gathered to it—so long as the idea of the unity of God's government was fresh and living—felt empowered as His servants to execute His will upon earth.

A religion stands or falls with its idea of God. Now Mohammed claims that his idea of God is the Christian idea purified. "Say ye to the Christians," he says, "their God and my God is one." But, in point of fact, the peculiar contents of the Christian revelation are discarded, and the God of Mohammed is a God exalted indeed and mighty, but remote and awful, devoid of the subduing, uplifting, holy love, of which nothing save the Incarnation conveys an adequate knowledge, or gives the needed proof. Very spirited and true are the terms in which he frequently describes God: "God! there is no God but He—the Living, the Self-subsisting; neither slumber seizeth Him, nor sleep: all that is in the heavens and in the earth is His. Who is he that can intercede with Him but by His own permission? He knoweth what is present with His creatures, and what is yet to befall them; yet nought of His knowledge do they comprehend, save what He willeth. His throne reacheth over the heavens and the earth, and the upholding of both burdeneth Him not. And He is the High, the Great."[1] But, like every other system of Deism, Mohammedanism fails to convey to our

[1] Sura ii. 256.

minds the idea of a God perfect in love and in purity, as well as in power. Between Allah and His creatures there remains a deep and impassable gulf. Dean Milman has, with his wonted precision, indicated the radical defect of this idea of God, when he says: "The absorption into, or even the approximation towards, the Deity, by contemplation in this life, or perfection in the life to come, are equally foreign to the Koran."[1] The sterner virtues may be cultivated under the light of such knowledge of God as Mohammed proclaimed; but it requires the penetrating warmth of a Divine and holy love, pressing on to perfect intimacy with His creatures, to fertilize that inmost soil of the heart where the roots of what is tender, humble, and self-sacrificing, draw their nutriment. Mohammed indeed presents to us a God not only mighty, as is sometimes alleged, but also holy and forgiving. Every verse of the Koran is given "in the name of God, the Compassionate, the Merciful;" but this compassion is exhibited much more in a lenient indulgence to the infirmities of men, than in making provision for their deliverance from them. "God desireth to make your burden light to you, for man hath been created weak." This is the refrain of that notable Sura[2] in

[1] *Latin Christianity*, ii. 192. [2] Sura iv.

which such liberal allowance is made for the appetites and errors of the followers of Mohammed. "God is knowing, wise:" this is the constantly reiterated ground of man's confidence. God knows how weak human nature is, He understands the violence of appetite, and does not expect perfect purity.[1] This considerate, indulgent God, who makes no provision for assimilating men to Himself, is very different from the God of Christ, whose welcome, all-hopeful summons is, Be ye holy, for I am holy, perfect as your Father in heaven is perfect. Indeed, the defects of Mohammed's idea of God suggest to us to inquire whether it is possible to conceive worthily of God's holiness, except by seeing it expressed in a perfectly holy human life, or of His love, except by seeing God incarnate, emptying Himself, and as a man dying for men, that they may be one with Him for ever.

Now recent investigation has brought out with considerable clearness that the Semitic conception of God is essentially distinct from the Aryan idea.[2] The Aryan races have everywhere shown a tendency to think of God, and to name Him through His works. They have recognised the beneficent influence of the sun

[1] See the profound remarks of Mozley, *Bampton Lectures*, pp. 178–181.

[2] Fairbairn's *Studies*, p. 316.

and the rain; they have trembled before the hurricane; and feeling that these forces of nature were uncontrollable by themselves, they have either worshipped them or have prayed to some Spirit who overruled them. Their tendency has been to find and worship the Creator in the creature. The distinction between the two has been obliterated, and the interval between heaven and earth filled up. In the luxuriant mythology of Greece, it is impossible to say where the Divine ends and the human begins: gods become men, and men become gods. In the pantheism of the Aryans of India, it is as difficult to disentangle the human from the Divine. And, therefore, as has been observed, the idea of the Incarnation was akin to the Aryan conception of God; but it was most repugnant and antagonistic to the Semitic mind, which conceived of God as the infinitely exalted Sovereign, which named its God, the Lord, the King, the Mighty One. Mohammed's idea of God was, therefore, essentially the Semitic idea. He, as little as the great bulk of the Jews themselves, could not bring his mind to accept the Incarnation or fill up the abyss between God and man. As has been said by the writer who has most clearly elucidated this point: "It is of the essence of Christianity to affirm the Fatherhood of God. It is of the essence of Mohammedanism to deny the Fatherhood of God. The quarrel between Mohammedans and Christians is not, as Mr. Bosworth Smith says, a quarrel between near relations, but a quarrel between sons and servants."[1]

"One God the Arabian Prophet preached to man,
One God the Orient still
Adores through many a mighty span,
A God of Power and Will.

A God that, shrouded in His lonely light,
Rests utterly apart
From all the vast creations of His might,
From Nature, Man, and Art."

The baldness and onesidedness of the Mohammedan confession have received melancholy illustration throughout the whole history of Islam. It has been a religion of opposition from the first, living by aggression, mighty and purifying while it flows in full flood, but when resting and at peace, it stagnates and throws up a filthy and putrid scum. As a battle-cry none is more animating and invigorating than "There is no God but God;" everything to which we are opposed is as stubble before the fire; already the day is ours, because we fight the battles of the One God. But when the victory is won, and men have to shape a life of

[1] Dr. Robson, *British and Foreign Evangelical Review*, Jan. 1877.

peace for themselves, there is nothing in this creed to guide or to sustain. "Hence," says Mr. Maurice, "it has been proved that Mahometanism can only thrive while it is aiming at conquest. Why? Because it is the proclamation of a mere sovereign, who employs men to declare the fact that he is a sovereign, and to enforce it upon the world. It is not the proclamation of a great moral Being, who deigns to raise His creatures out of their sensual and natural degradation; who reveals to them not merely that He is, but *what* He is—why He has created them—what they have to do with Him. Unless this mighty chasm in the Mahometan doctrine can be filled up, it must wither day by day—wither for all purposes of utility to mankind; it can leave nothing behind but a wretched carcase, filling the air with the infection of its rottenness."[1] Similarly writes one who viewed Mohammedanism from a totally different point of view.[2] "So long as a Mahometan nation is dominant and conquering, so long is it great and glorious after its own standard. When it ceases to have an enemy to contend against, it sinks into sluggish stupidity and into a barbarism far viler than that of the conquerors who raised it to greatness."

[1] *Religions of the World*, p. 28.

[2] Freeman's *Lectures*, p. 202 (2nd ed.).

But that which differentiates Moslems from all other deists, is their belief that Mohammed is the prophet of God. This indeed may not seem an astounding nor an unwarranted claim, when we learn that they recognise 224,000, or, according to a more moderate computation, 124,000 prophets;[1] and that even Mohammed himself seemed to consider not only Lôkman the Sage—the Arabian Æsop—but even Alexander the Great, a prophet of God. But of these prophets six have been the bearers of new laws and revelations, which superseded all that had been delivered by their predecessors. These six are Adam, Noah, Abraham, Moses, Jesus, and Mohammed. Mohammed, coming last, is entitled the "Seal of the Prophets,"[2] summing up and closing all the revelations of God. Mohammed believed in the miraculous conception of our Lord, in the miracles of Moses and other prophets, and in the Jewish and Christian Scriptures; but had he known with accuracy the contents of previous revelations, he would never have appeared in the character of the final prophet. His knowledge of Christianity is so meagre and confused, that it is difficult to understand how even the most illiterate and mystified sectary fed on apocryphal gospels

[1] Hughes's *Notes on Muhammadanism*, p. 51. Reland, p. 41.

[2] Sura lxxxiii. 40.

could have conveyed to him such notions of the Gospel. Of the great and enlightening history of Israel, as a history, he knows nothing, and has merely caught up some childish tales from the Talmud and some garbled legends of the Hebrew patriarchs and great men.[1] This last of the prophets firmly believed that the Old and New Testament Scriptures were from God, and yet he took no pains to ascertain what they had revealed. He enjoined on his followers, on pain of eternal punishment, to believe in these Scriptures as well as in the Koran, and yet he did not know what he was commanding them to believe. He has by this ignorance involved himself and all his followers in a fatal inconsistency. The Koran everywhere attributes inspiration and a Divine origin to the Scriptures as emphatically as it claims these for itself; while at the same time it is impossible for a believer in the Scriptures to believe in the Koran. "This Koran," it says,[2] "could not have been composed by any except God! but it is a confirmation of that which was revealed before it." Again, "There is no God but God, the living, the self-subsisting; He hath sent

[1] This was apparently urged against Mohammed even by his contemporaries. See *Koran*, Sura xvi. 26: "When it is said unto them, What hath the Lord sent down to Mohammed? they answer, Ancient fables."

[2] Sura x.

down unto thee the book of the Koran with truth, confirming that which was revealed before it, for He had formerly sent down the Law and the Gospel, a direction unto men."[1] Again, unbelief in the Scriptures is by Mohammed put on a level with unbelief in the Koran itself, as in the 40th Sura, where he says: "They who charge with falsehood the book of the Koran and the other sacred Scriptures and revealed doctrines which we sent our former apostles to preach, shall hereafter know their folly, when the collars shall be on their necks, and the chains by which they shall be dragged into hell."

Mohammedans, therefore, are in the awkward predicament of being obliged by their religion to believe in what explodes their religion. They are commanded to believe in two contradictories. They are commanded to accept Jesus as a prophet, and at the same time to accept Mohammed. They are enjoined to receive the Old Testament Scriptures as a revelation, although nothing is more obvious in these Scriptures than that the history of Judaism developes into and finds its completion and end in Christianity; and they are enjoined to believe in the New Testament Scriptures, although these writings so distinctly claim to be the final

[1] Sura iii. 1.

revelation, that it is impossible to find room for the claims of Mohammed as the ultimate revealer of God's will. It is this inconsistent demand of their creed which produces those anomalies in the conduct of Moslems, so astonishing to those who expect to find only hatred of everything Christian. Lady Duff Gordon records that the Moslem carpenter she employed was seen swallowing the sawdust of the cedar he was using for his work, because that was the tree under which Mary had sat with Jesus during the flight into Egypt.[1] Under Moslem governments men have been put to death for blaspheming the name of Jesus. And according to their own divines, "every Alim (or doctor of the law) should read the Towrat and the Ingeel (*i.e.*, the Law and the Gospel); the words of Seyiddna Eesa are the true faith."[2]

Neither can they evade the awkwardness of this false position by propounding that the later revelation supersedes the earlier, and that they receive the words of Jesus only in so far as these are confirmed by the words of Mohammed. This may apply in so far as the New Testament is a code, but in so far as it is a history, it has no application. Earlier precepts or laws

[1] *Last Letters*, p. 66; and *Letters*, p. 82.
[2] Ibid. p. 206. Comp. Wood's *Oxus*, p. 301.

may be repealed or superseded by later precepts, but facts cannot be cancelled from past history.[1] If the facts recorded in the Gospels are true, then there is no room for Mohammed in the world. And, in point of fact, instructed Moslems recognise their dilemma, and universally maintain that our Scriptures are corrupted;[2] that is to say, the ultimate defence of Mohammedanism is one which a single whiff of European criticism will blow to the winds.

But is Mohammed in no sense a prophet? Certainly he had two of the most important characteristics of the prophetic order. He saw truth about God which his fellow-men did not see, and he had an irresistible inward impulse to publish this truth. In respect of this latter qualification Mohammed may stand comparison with the most courageous of the heroic prophets of Israel. For the truth's sake he risked his life, he suffered daily persecution for years, and eventually banishment, the loss of property, of the goodwill of his fellow-citizens, and of the

[1] "If you believe in the Gospel as inspired, you may indeed alter its precepts by the Coran, but you cannot cancel the fact of Christ's death." p. xii. of *The Testimony borne by the Coran to the Jewish and Christian Scriptures.* 2nd edition, published anonymously by Sir William Muir, at Allahabad, 1860.

[2] Henry Martyn, *Controversial Tracts on Christianity and Mohammedanism.* Edited by Dr. S. Lee, Cambridge, 1824.

confidence of his friends—he suffered, in short, as much as any man can suffer short of death, which he only escaped by flight, and yet he unflinchingly proclaimed his message. No bribe, threat, or inducement could silence him. "Though they array against me the sun on the right hand and the moon on the left, I cannot renounce my purpose." And it was this persistency, this belief in his call to proclaim the unity of God, which was the making of Islam. Other men have been monotheists in the midst of idolaters, but no other man has founded a strong and enduring monotheistic religion. The distinction in his case was his resolution that other men should believe. If we ask what it was that made Mohammed aggressive and proselytizing where other men had been content to cherish a solitary faith, we must answer that it was nothing else than the depth and force of his own conviction of the truth. To himself the difference between one God and many, between the unseen Creator and these ugly lumps of stone or wood, was simply infinite. The one creed was death and darkness to him, the other light and life. It is useless seeking for motives in such a case—for ends to serve and selfish reasons for his speaking: the impossibility with Mohammed was to keep silence. His acceptance of the office of teacher of his people was anything but the ill-advised and sudden impulse of a light-minded vanity or ambition. His own convictions had been reached only after long years of lonely mental agony, and of a doubt and distraction bordering on madness. Who can doubt the earnestness of that search after truth and the living God, that drove the affluent merchant from his comfortable home and his fond wife, to make his abode for months at a time in the dismal cave on Mount Hira? If we respect the shrinking of Isaiah or Jeremiah from the heavy task of proclaiming unwelcome truth, we must also respect the keen sensitiveness of Mohammed, who was so burdened by this same responsibility, and so persuaded of his incompetency for the task, that at times he thought his new feelings and thoughts were a snare of the devil, and at times he would fain have rid himself of all further struggle by casting himself from a friendly precipice. His rolling his head in his mantle, the sound of the ringing of bells in his ears, his sobbing like a young camel, the sudden grey hairs which he himself ascribed to the terrific Suras,—what were all these but so many physical signs of a nervous organization overstrained by anxiety and thought?

His giving himself out as a prophet of God was, in the first instance, not only sincere, but probably correct in the sense in which he himself understood it. He felt that he had thoughts of God which it deeply concerned all around him to receive, and he knew that these thoughts were given him by God, although not, as we shall see, a revelation strictly so called. His mistake by no means lay in his supposing himself to be called upon by God to speak for Him and introduce a better religion, but it lay in his gradually coming to insist quite as much on men's accepting him as a prophet as on their accepting the great truth he preached. He was a prophet to his countrymen in so far as he proclaimed the unity of God, but this was no sufficient ground for his claiming to be their guide in all matters of religion, still less for his assuming the lordship over them in all matters civil as well. The modesty and humility apparent in him so long as his mind was possessed with objective truth, gradually gives way to the presumptuousness and arrogance of a mind turned more to a sense of its own importance. To put the second article of the Mohammedan creed on the same level as the first, to make it as essential that men should believe in the mission of Mohammed as in the unity of God, was no doubt the making of Islam, but it was an ignorant, incongruous, and false combination.

Had Mohammed known his own ignorance as well as his knowledge, the world would have had one religion the less, and Christianity would have had one more reformer.

But when it is asked, Was Mohammed sincere throughout? I believe there is no question in religious biography more difficult to answer. There need, I think, be no question about his original sincerity. Trained like another Samuel under the shadow of the temple of which his ancestors were the guardians, alone allowed to sit with his grandfather on his prayer-rug in the temple-court,[1] prized by that aged chief as the jewel of all his tribe, it was only to be expected that he should grow up with a strong religious bent. It is a striking proof of his sincerity that his earliest and most devoted disciples were those of his own household, and his familiars, who had known him in all circumstances and scanned him in all moods—his wife, his slave, his cousin, his father-in-law—the latter themselves men of character and position. Neither is it credible that a man who was seeking to impose on the public should have distinctly asserted that he could not command the spirit of inspiration, and should have waited for six months or two years for communications which he very ur-

[1] Caussin de Perceval's *Hist. des Arabes*, i. 289.

gently needed. So far from being a common impostor, he showed himself superior to the kind of temptation to which the leader of a crowd of admiring disciples is most exposed. On the saddest day of Mohammed's life, when the light of it seemed to have gone down in the grave of his little boy Ibrahim, an eclipse of the sun occurred as he went home, and his friends spoke of it as a kind of token of the sympathy of Heaven. A vulgar impostor would have accepted the flattery, but Mohammed simply said, "The sun and the moon are amongst the signs appointed by the Lord. They are not eclipsed on the death of any one."[1] His correspondence with the rival prophet, Moseilama, has commonly and justly been cited as exhibiting the difference between the impostor and the true man. It ran thus: "Moseilama, the Apostle of God, to Mohammed, the Apostle of God. Now let the earth be half mine and half thine." "Mohammed, the Apostle of God, to Moseilama, the Liar. The earth is God's; He giveth it for inheritance to such of His servants as He pleaseth, and the happy issue shall attend those that fear Him."

The difficulty is to reconcile with this sincerity acts which certainly at first sight one is tempted to condemn as immoral and dishonest.

[1] Muir, iv. 166.

Instead of feeling it to be incumbent on him as a prophet of God to set his followers an example of temperance and high-toned living, he rather used his office as a title to license from which ordinary men were restrained. Restricting his disciples to four wives, he retained to himself the liberty of taking as many as he pleased. He actually married eleven women, nine of whom survived him. And this he sanctions by publishing a new paragraph of the Koran, as allowing him this "privilege above the rest of the faithful."[1] One is tempted to exclaim, with honest old Hoornbeek, "Dignum certe Propheta privilegium."[2] Yet let us make what allowance is possible. So long as Kadijah lived Mohammed was a strict monogamist. Until he was fifty-three years of age he showed no disposition to adopt the custom of his country, and his unmarried youth had been exceptionally pure. But the sons Kadijah bore him died in infancy, and his enemies taunted him in most offensive terms with his lack of a male heir. Besides this, we must take into account that among Oriental chiefs and princes the extension of the harem has always been one of the first modes of exhibiting the grandeur of a ruler. We remember the as-

[1] Sura xxxiii. 48.

[2] Hoornbeek, *Summa Controv.* p. 107.

tounding number of Solomon's wives—a number far exceeded by many of Mohammed's successors. Something, too, must be allowed for his desire to form good alliances and to provide for the widows of his devoted followers. All his wives but one were widows, and many of them were possibly added to his harem as a mode of showing respect for the dead, and of providing the widows with what was considered an honourable pension. But this does not account for all his marriages, and least of all does it account for his scandalous ámours; and I am of opinion that after Kadijah's influence was withdrawn, his relations with women were of a thoroughly discreditable kind. His morality at this point was not that of a high-minded or spiritual man, it was not that of a man whose religion had exercised a purifying influence upon him,—it was no higher than that of his contemporaries, and it was immensely lower than that of Christian countries.

But all this might have been overlooked. The knot of the matter lies not in his polygamy, nor even in his occasional licentiousness, but in the fact that he defended his conduct, when it created scandal, by professed revelations which are now embodied as parts of the Koran. When his wives murmured, and with justice, at his irregularities, he silenced them by a revelation giving him conjugal allowances which he had himself proscribed as unlawful. When he designed to contract an alliance with a woman forbidden to him by his own law, an inspired permission was forthcoming, encouraging him to the transgression. I fear that, notwithstanding all that has been urged in explanation, the common sense of every Christian community will pronounce that underneath this kind of conduct a low *morale* must have existed. It is idle to dismiss the question as Carlyle does with the exclamation, "A false man found a religion? Why, a false man cannot build a brick house!" For my part, I'd as soon go with Thackeray, when he says: "A lie once set agoing, having the breath of life breathed into it by the father of lying, and ordered to run its diabolical little course, lives with a prodigious vitality. You say, 'Magna est veritas et prævalebit.' Psha! Great lies are as great as great truths, and prevail constantly, and day after day."

But of late years the idea has been gaining ground that Mohammed was not only sincere in his zeal for religion, but was also sincere in his conviction that the revelations above referred to were from God. The great name of Möhler is cited as an advocate of this opinion, and, what is much more, as one who attempts to explain the state of mind in which Mohammed could suppose that immoral precepts were the inspiration of God. "I maintain," he says, "that if one admits the possibility of any man's being able to give out his own individual religious impressions, ideas, and thoughts, without suspicion, for divine inspirations, I cannot perceive the impossibility of his considering God also to be the author of all his other inward impulses." It is possible, that is to say, to suppose that Mohammed considered that God was the author of his impulse to lust after other men's wives, and to break his promise in order to gratify his appetites. If so, then his conscience was in a state of obfuscation not surpassed by the wildest anabaptists or fanatics of any age, and wholly unfitting him to be a teacher or ruler of men.

I believe, however, that Mohammed had been so much in the habit of promulgating laws and issuing manifestoes in the capacity of God's apostle, that he had ceased on each occasion to consider whether he was merely speaking for God's cause, or was speaking God's word. I believe that, situated as he was, he could not fail at length to act on the understanding that his commission as God's apostle was a general one, and that he did not need to wait on each occasion for what he could distinctly recognise as a revelation.[1] He had to speak and to act on the spot for the present emergency, and being God's apostle, his word was God's word. And this no doubt made the final step easier. Pressed by strong temptation, entangled in circumstances that threatened to diminish his influence, he boldly used, for his own purposes, the method and authority he had so often used for the government of the cause of Islam. But that he did so without compunction I do not believe. Nor do I believe that had he accomplished the desire expressed on his death-bed of revising the Koran, he would have allowed these parts of it to remain, if even he meant that they should ever be published to the world. But in whatever way these matters are explained, Mohammed appears in them a man of a much lower type than the Old Testament prophets, not to speak of such men as Paul or John.

The strength of Mohammed's conviction is best measured by its results in those around him. It has been said that the best proof a

[1] Pfleiderer's opinion is that the specification of God as the author of each revelation had become a form of speech : "Es ist das kaum anders zu beurtheilen als die Phraseologie unseres Konversationsstyls, wo ja die Unächtheit der kursirenden Phrasen darum schon unschuldig ist, weil Jedermann sie kennt."—*Die Religion* ii. 369.

prophet can give of the authenticity of his mission is to win credence to it.[1] Certainly Mohammed gave this proof, and thereby evinced, if not the authenticity of his mission, yet his own belief in it. With admirable sagacity and sincerity he declined to give himself out as a worker of miracles. To those who asked for signs, he replied, "Signs are in the power of God alone, and I am no more than a public preacher."[2] Other prophets had come with miracles, and had been disbelieved,[3] therefore Mohammed came with the sword. Those whom God had ordained to believe would believe without miracles, and no miracles would convince the rest. And yet, with all this disclaiming of miracle, Mohammed most emphatically asserted the existence of a continuous miracle in the Koran. "We have not sent any before thee as our apostles, other than men unto whom we spake by revelation. . . . We sent them with evident miracles, and written revelations, and we have sent down unto thee this Koran."[4] Again and again he appeals to the Koran as the standing proof of his mission, and challenges the world to produce anything equal to it. "If ye be in doubt

[1] Oelsner, *Effets*, &c., p. 35: "La meilleure preuve qu'un prophète puisse donner de l'authenticité de sa mission, c'est d'y faire croire."

[2] Sura xxix. 49. [3] Sura vi. *passim*. [4] Sura xvi. 45.

concerning that revelation which we have sent down unto our servant, produce a chapter like unto it."[1] So that the more enthusiastic of the Mohammedans have been accustomed to claim for their prophet a pre-eminence in regard to miracles. Sixty thousand is the number of the miracles he wrought, each verse of the Koran being itself a miracle. And he alone of the prophets has wrought a permanent and standing miracle, in the Koran, which all generations may for themselves examine.[2]

As regards the practice enjoined upon Mohammedans, Islam is commonly said to rest upon five pillars or foundations,[3] viz., 1. The recital of the Kalima, or confession: There is but one God, and Mohammed is His prophet; 2. Observance of the five daily periods of prayer; 3. The giving of alms; 4. The fast of Ramadan; and 5. Pilgrimage to Mecca. In these practical duties, there is nothing very different from Judaism, or, if we except pilgrimage, from Christianity. The times and forms of prayer are certainly more generally observed among Mohammedans than among ourselves. From the first call to prayer in the early morning,

Sura ii. 21, and xvii. 91.

[2] Pocock, *Specimen*, p. 192; Gagnier, *Vie de Mahomet*, ii. 367.

[3] Reland, *De Rel. Moh.* p. 5.

when the sleepers are roused by the sonorous and musical cry of the Muezzin, "Prayer is better than sleep," through all the throng and business of the day, wherever and in whatever engaged, at each hour of prayer the Mohammedan drops his tools or lays aside his pipe, and prostrates himself towards Mecca.

There are two features of the devout character which the Mohammedans have the merit of exhibiting with much greater distinctness than we do. They show not the smallest hesitation or fear in confessing God, and they reduce to practice the great principle that the worship of God is not confined to temples or any special place :—

> "Most honour to the men of prayer,
> Whose mosque is in them everywhere!
> Who, amid revel's wildest din,
> In war's severest discipline,
> On rolling deck, in thronged bazaar,
> In stranger land, however far,
> However different in their reach
> Of thought, in manners, dress, or speech,—
> Will quietly their carpet spread,
> To Mekkeh turn the humble head,
> And, as if blind to all around,
> And deaf to each distracting sound,
> In ritual language God adore,
> In spirit to His presence soar,
> And, in the pauses of the prayer,
> Rest, as if rapt in glory there."

There are of course formalists and hypocrites in

Islam as well as in religions of which we have more experience. The uniformity and regularity of their prostrations resemble the movements of a well-drilled company of soldiers, or of machines, but the Koran[1] denounces "woe upon those who pray, but in their prayers are careless; who make a show of devotion, but refuse to help the needy;" while nowhere is formalism more pungently ridiculed than in the common Arabic proverb, "His head is towards the Kibleh, but his heels are among the weeds."[2] We could almost excuse a touch of formalism for the sake of securing that absolute stillness and outward decorum in worship which deceives the stranger as he enters a crowded mosque into the belief that it is quite empty.[3] Persons who hold themselves excused from the duty of worship by every slight obstacle might do worse than get infected with the sublime formalism of Cais, son of Sad, who would not shift his head an inch from the place of his prostration, though a huge serpent lifted its fangs close to his face and finally coiled itself round his neck.[4] And if some are formal, certainly many are very much in earnest.[5] It is

[1] Sura cvii. [2] Burckhardt's *Arabic. Prov.* p. 97.

[3] Hottinger, *Hist. Orient.* p. 310.

[4] Dozy's *Histoire*, i. 66.

[5] "Etliche beten und rufen in ihren Häusern mit solchem Eifer und so lange bis ihnen der Odem entgehet,

only fair, in forming a judgment of the devotional element in Mohammedanism, to have before us such a prayer as this: "O Lord, I supplicate Thee for firmness in faith, and direction towards rectitude, and to assist me in being grateful to Thee, and in adoring Thee in every good way; and I supplicate Thee for an innocent heart, which shall not incline to wickedness; and I supplicate Thee for a true tongue, and for that virtue which Thou knowest; and I pray Thee to defend me from that vice which Thou knowest; and for forgiveness of those faults which Thou knowest. O my defender! assist me in remembering Thee, and being grateful to Thee, and in worshipping Thee with the excess of my strength. O Lord! I have injured my own soul, and no one can pardon the faults of Thy servants but Thou. Forgive me out of Thy lovingkindness, and have mercy on me; for verily Thou art the forgiver of offences, and the bestower of blessings upon Thy servants."[1]

But the attachment of the Moslems to their religion is put to a severer test by the fast of Ramadan. This fast is no make-believe, no abstinence during a hot month from the heavier articles of food to whet the appetite for the

und sie gleichsam in Ohnmacht niedersinken."—Olcarius, quoted in Pfeiffer, p. 418.

[1] Syed Ali, *Crit. Exam.* p. 175.

lighter efforts of cookery; but it is a *bonâ-fide* total abstinence from food, drink, and smoking from sunrise to sunset of each day throughout the whole month of the Mohammedan Lent. From half-past two in the morning, or whenever the gun gives the signal in the larger cities, till the happy and eagerly looked-for release of sundown, nothing may pass over the throat. The hard-wrought labourer in the burning streets or under the terrific blaze of the Eastern noon must endure his faintness and misery unrelieved by a single mouthful of water. The traveller in the desert may be blinded with the glare of the brazen sky above and the glowing sand beneath, he may fall from the back of his camel or sit insensible in the saddle, but he may chew nothing, taste nothing, if possible not even smell what might for the moment revive his failing energy. Even in illness this fast is kept, although that is not obligatory. Burton says, "I found but one patient who would eat, even to save his life. And among the vulgar, sinners who habitually drink when they should pray will fast and perform their devotions through the Ramadan."[1] It is not surprising that the expiry of this compulsory fast should be hailed with all the manifestations of intense satisfaction and re-

[1] Burton, *Pilgrim.* i. 109.

lief. Drums are beat, every one who has a gun or pistol contributes to the roar of jubilation, while the very children, aware how much more facile the parental temper will now be, go about shouting, "*Ramadan mat*," Ramadan is dead.[1] The most obvious, if not the most real and permanent, effect of this "blessed month" is to spoil the tempers of the whole community. A hungry man is an angry man all the world over, and though fasting has its spiritual uses in certain cases, this compulsory abstinence of a whole population produces irritability, quarrelsomeness, and all the ills of dyspepsia. But it will of course be understood that the better instructed and the pious Moslems recognise the necessity of using the season of fast for spiritual discipline.[2] "God cares not," says the Mishcat, "that a man leave off eating and drinking, if he do not therewith abandon lying and detraction."[3]

Great stress is laid upon almsgiving. "A liberal unbeliever," says Ali,[4] "may sooner hope for Paradise than an avaricious Mohammedan." Islam has been greatly commended for the provision it makes for the poor. The

[1] Lady Duff Gordon's *Letters*, p. 217.
[2] Pocock's *Specimen*, p. 310.
[3] Mill's *Hist. of Mohammedanism*, p. 311.
[4] Forster's *Mahom. Unveiled*, i. 346.

only criticism which one is disposed to pass upon its law of almsgiving is a criticism which applies to many other parts of the religion, and that is, that it leaves too little to the spirit and spontaneity of the individual, and too definitely prescribes and enforces duty. The *Zakat*, or legal alms, is collected by Government in Mohammedan countries, and, like our income tax, is exacted only from those who have a certain amount of revenue and have been in possession of the same for a year. Of all his property, the Moslem must give a prescribed portion, one-tenth of grain or fruit, one of every hundred camels, 2½ per cent. of his money, both capital and profits. And the amount thus contributed is applied to the relief of debtors who cannot pay their debts, for the aid of slaves who wish to buy their freedom, of strangers, travellers, pilgrims, and destitute persons.[1] And it is the judgment of one who has observed the working of this law in Mohammedan countries, and is nowise prejudiced in favour of Islam, that "whatever be the weak points in Mohammedanism, all candid observers acquainted with the condition of Mohammedan nations must admit that its provision for the poor is highly commendable. As we have journeyed from village to village

[1] Sura ix. 60.

among the Afghans, we have frequently been struck with the absence of great poverty, and even in our large cities, where Mohammedan beggars are numerous, it must be remembered that they are either religious mendicants or professional beggars, and for the most part quite unworthy of charitable relief."[1]

The fourth point of Mohammedan practice is pilgrimage. Every Moslem, male or female, and in whatever country resident, must at least once visit the Holy City and Temple of Mecca. This duty is enjoined in the Koran; it is enforced by the example of Mohammed himself, and by a traditional saying of his, to the effect that he who dies without performing it may as well die a Jew or a Christian. A dying man may, however, bequeath a sufficient sum of money to pay the expenses of a deputy-pilgrim,[2] so that his personal neglect may be repaired. The words of the Koran regarding pilgrimage admit of some latitude of interpretation: "It is a duty towards God incumbent on those who are able to go thither, to visit the house of God."[3] But who are those who are able? The straiter sects say: Every one who is able to walk and to earn his bread on the way; and,

[1] Hughes, Notes, p. 85.

[2] Hughes (*Notes*, pp. 91, 92) denies that proxies are allowable during the principal's lifetime.

[3] Sura iii.; cf. also Sura xxii.

consequently, many poor creatures leave their homes in Northern India or inner Africa, resolved to beg their way to Mecca, and face all the terrors of the desert, the sea, and foreign countries. The most reasonable teachers, however, maintain that pilgrimage is incumbent only on such as have money for the road and for the support of their families during their absence.[1] And as the minimum expenditure of a man who rides in a litter from Damascus and back is about £1200, it cannot surprise us if a large proportion of the Moslem population plead inability to comply with this demand of their Prophet. "Going on pilgrimage to Mecca," says the first Englishman who ever went there, "is a duty incumbent on every Mussulman, if in capacity of health and purse, but yet a great many who are so live in the final neglect of it."[2] The license given by the Koran[3] to use the pilgrimage for purposes of trade does not serve materially to increase the size of the caravans. And although pauper pilgrims are provided by the government with a gratis sea passage, and

[1] Burton's *Pilgrimage*, iii. 224.

[2] Joseph Pitts' *Faithful Account*, p. 84.

[3] Sura ii: "It shall be no crime in you if ye seek an increase from the Lord, by trading during the pilgrimage." Burton's judgment is that the pilgrimage is "essentially religious, accidentally an affair of commerce" (*Pilgrimage*, iii. 225).

frequently have their expenses paid by wealthy men who desire the credit of a meritorious act, the numbers in 1853 were only 50,000, and seemed then to be steadily decreasing.[1] Since then, however, they have increased threefold.

Mecca is the Holy City of Islam, not because it is the birthplace of Mohammed, but because it contains the most ancient temple in Arabia, the world-renowned Kaabah, or Bait-Allah.[2] Of this temple the Koran boldly says: "Verily, the first house appointed unto man to worship in was that which is in Becca, blessed, and the Keblah for all creatures. Therein are manifest signs:[3] the place where Abraham stood; and whosoever entereth therein shall be safe." This dictum was evoked in correction of the Jewish idea, that Jerusalem was the true Keblah, towards which all worshippers should pray—an idea with which, remarkably enough, Mohammed himself had at first fallen in. And enlightened Moham-

[1] "Ali Bey (A.D. 1807) calculates 83,000 pilgrims; Burckhardt (1814) 70,000. I reduced it, in 1853, to 50,000." Burton, iii. 259.

[2] Burton (iii. 149) says that Bait-Ullah and Kaabah are synonymous. So too Sale, *Preliminary Discourse*, p. 88. Hughes (*Notes*, 88) says that this is a confusion, and appropriates the name Bait-Ullah to the whole mosque, and not distinctively to the Kaabah.

[3] The fullest account of these signs is given by Boulainvilliers, *La Vie de Mahomed*, pp. 84–91.

medans of the present day, while they reject the legends which ascribe to this temple a supernatural origin and a date anterior to the Creation, agree in believing that it was originally built by Abraham and Ishmael. For this there is no evidence but that of tradition, and the fact that the chief object of veneration in it is a stone which is claimed as a relic of patriarchal worship. Of its great antiquity there is no doubt. Not only is it recognised as a holy city by four different faiths, the Hindu, Sabæan, Gueber, and Moslem;[1] but even before the Christian era it was well known as an ancient and revered temple.[2] The Kaabah stands in a wide court, skirted by colonnades of marble and stone pillars, and ornamented by a number of domes, and is itself, as its name denotes, in the form of a *cube* of about thirty-five feet.[3] Built into its north-east corner, about four or five feet from the ground, is the famous "Black Stone,"[4] which sober Moslems believe to have been brought from a neighbouring mountain to mark the point from which the circumambulation of the

[1] Burton, iii. 160.

[2] Diodorus Sic. iii. 44.

[3] For exact measurements and description, see Burton's third volume, p. 149, *et seq.;* or Sale's *Prelim. Disc.*, p. 88.

[4] About eight inches long by six in height. See Muir's plate in vol. ii.

Kaabah was to commence, but which enthusiasts believe to have fallen from heaven,[1] and to be destined to witness at the last day in favour of all those who have kissed it. Originally white, it is supposed to have become black by the kisses of sinful men. Close by is the well *Zem-Zem*, to which, according to Arabian ideas, all Moslems owe their being, for it was here that the despairing Hagar found water to restore their great ancestor.[2]

Here also is the burial-place of Hagar and Ishmael, marked by a slab for the veneration of believers. And in the small building, called Makam Ibrahim, is the stone which served Abraham as a platform while building the Kaabah, and which retains the print of his feet. The Kaabah itself is covered with a brilliant black cloth, called the Kiswah, which is annually renewed by the Sultan, and on which are inscribed portions of the Koran.[3]

When the pilgrim arrives at the last stage on

[1] "It appeared to me," says Burton (iii. p. 158) "a common aerolite." See Syed Ahmed's *Essay on the History of Mecca*, where a pretty view of the Kaabah is given.

[2] It was Mohammed's grandfather, the guardian of the Kaabah, who first formed a well for the storing of this water.

[3] Described in Burton, iii. 295–9; and cf. Lane's *Modern Egyptians*, ii. 213. Burton considers that the origin of the veiling of the Kaabah must be sought "in the ancient practice of typifying the Church visible by a virgin or bride." This seems unlikely. Van Lennep,

his way to Mecca, about five miles from the town, he enters the sacred territory. Here, accordingly, he bathes, lays aside his clothes, and assumes the proper pilgrim garb (Ihram), which consists of two unstitched white cotton cloths, one of which is wrapped round the waist, while the other is thrown over the shoulders. This, with sandals, is the only covering of the pilgrim. On arriving at the sacred building itself, the pilgrim prays, drinks a cup of the distasteful water of Zem-Zem, and begins his circumambulation, or *Tawaf*.[1] Seven times he makes the circuit of the Kaabah, keeping his left side next it, uttering prayers and acts of adoration as he goes. The first three circuits are made with impetuous movements, as of one making his way against difficulties, asserting his belief in the face of an opposing world;[2] the remaining circuits are made with the usual ease

(*Bible Lands*, ii. 717) thinks it indicates its connection with a people dwelling in tents. The old Kiswah is sold piecemeal by the officials. It is much used for book-markers for Korans, and as charms. Waistcoats made of it make the wearer invulnerable.

[1] Some Arabic writers connect this circumambulation with the motions of the heavenly bodies, affirming that men should resemble these, not only in purity, but in their circular motion. Sale's *Preliminary Discourse*, p. 93; *Burton*, iii. 205. Reland, *De Rel. Moh.* p. 123, quotes authorities to the same effect.

[2] "Ut se alacres futuros ostendant in certamine cum iis qui plures Deos colunt," says Reland, *De Rel. Moh.* p. 117.

of movement. The Black Stone is then kissed, the whole body pressed against the sacred edifice, and the pilgrim gives way to the thronging crowd that follows him. The other essentials of pilgrimage are the seven runs between the Mounts Safa and Marwah, the visit to Mount Arafat, the stoning of the devil, and the concluding sacrifice. Worn out with the exposure, the violent exertions, and the watching entailed by such ceremonies, the wearied pilgrim rests a few days and then proceeds homewards. On his arrival he is hailed as a distinguished person, his intercession is besought,[1] and he is ever after dignified by the title of Haji added to his name.

A recent English apologist for Mohammedanism has remarked that pilgrimage is "in theory and in reality alien alike to Mohammedanism and Christianity,"[2] and was merely a concession

[1] See Lane, ii. 157.

[2] Bosworth Smith, *Mohammed*, p. 164. Sale's remarks (*Preliminary Discourse*, p. 93) are well worth weighing: "The pilgrimage to Mecca, and the ceremonies prescribed to those who perform it, are, perhaps, liable to greater exception than any other of Mohammed's institutions; not only as silly and ridiculous in themselves, but as relics of idolatrous superstitions. Yet whoever seriously considers how difficult it is to make people submit to the abolishing of ancient customs, how unreasonable soever, which they are fond of, especially where the interest of a considerable party is also concerned, and that a man may with less danger change

to the natural weakness of his followers. And no doubt it is inconsistent with the spiritual sentiments which are found here and there in the Koran. Had pilgrimage not already existed, it would scarcely have been originated by him who said, "There is no piety in turning your faces towards the east or west, but he is pious who believeth in God, and the last day, and the angels, and the Scriptures, and the prophets; who giveth money for God's sake unto his kindred, and unto orphans, and the needy, and for redemption of captives; who is constant at prayers, and giveth alms; and of those who perform the covenant which they have covenanted, and who behave themselves patiently in adversity and hardships, and in times of violence; these are they who are true, and these are they who fear God."[1]

There seems to have always been among the best Mohammedans a feeling of something like apology, if not shame, in regard to this institution. Some of their leading theologians have been accustomed frankly to admit that the performances enjoined on the pilgrims have no intrinsic value, and make no appeal to the

many things than one great one, must excuse Mohammed's yielding some points of less moment to gain the principal."

[1] Sura ii.

reason, but they justify them on this very ground, pleading that obedience is never so disciplinary as when rendered blindly.[1] Omar himself is said to have uttered the following protest while doing obeisance to the black stone: "I know thou canst neither help nor hurt me, and unless I had seen the prophet do it, I would never have kissed thee." And Hakim, the mad Khalif of Egypt, tried to smash it with a club.[2] But the likelihood is that Mohammed, who himself belonged to what may be called the high-priestly family, believed that some peculiar sanctity attached to the Kaabah, and, knowing the advantages which accrued to his city from the annual influx of pilgrims, resolved to make pilgrimage obligatory on all his followers. And whether he foresaw the results of this injunction or not, there can be no doubt that in point of fact the influence of his religion has been vastly increased by this apparently absurd ceremonial. It is this which has stimulated the devotion of susceptible and imaginative minds; it is this which communicates to all Mohammedans an inspiring sense of the universality of their religion, and exhibits

[1] Algazali, quoted in Pocock's *Specimen*, pp. 312, 313, says, "Nihil hæc ad animum hominis, nec consentanea naturæ; . . . verum mandato simplici constant." Cf. Reland, *De Rel. Moh.* p. 122.

[2] Macbride's *Mohammedan Religion Explained*, p. 155.

in a form they can appreciate the unity of all believers.

What chiefly struck the young English sailor, who was compelled to apostatize, and in the capacity of a slave made the pilgrimage with his master two centuries ago, was the zeal which marked the worshippers who had journeyed for months, and possibly pinched for years to see Mecca ere they died. "It was a sight, indeed," he says, "able to pierce one's heart, to behold so many thousands in their garments of humility and mortification, with their naked heads and cheeks watered with tears; and to hear their grievous sighs and sobs, begging earnestly for the remission of their sins, and promising newness of life."[1] Burckhardt testifies to the same enthusiasm, and himself witnessed the emotion of an African, who, on reaching the Kaabah, burst into a flood of tears, and exclaimed, "O God, now take my soul, for this is paradise." And Captain Burton, a man not much given to emotion of any kind, acknowledges the impression made upon himself by the first sight of the bier-like Kaabah, and also by the simultaneous responses of thousands of pilgrims to the sermon in the temple-court. "I have seen," he says, "the religious ceremonies of many lands, but never

[1] Joseph Pitts' *Faithful Account*, p. 138.

—nowhere—aught so solemn, so impressive as this spectacle."[1] But more permanent than any religious or emotional impressions made by the worshipping multitudes on susceptible minds, is the influence of the visibility given at Mecca to the vastness and unity of the empire of Mohammed. It is here, where the Moor from the shores of the Mediterranean prostrates himself by the side of the Malay from the Southern Pacific, that the Mohammedans learn the extent of the prophet's dominion.[2] It is here they recognise the grandeur of the brotherhood Islam would fain introduce, as the wild Maghrabi and the Indian prince are seen kissing the stone together.[3] The pilgrim rites are foolish and indefensible, but, unmistakably, the maintenance of a local centre, as it was essential to Judaism,[4] has proved of incalculable service to Islam.

Four points in the theoretical and practical teaching of Mohammed have chiefly provoked criticism; the material and gross character of the heaven[5] he set before his followers, his

[1] Burton, iii. p. 316. Over against these manifestations of devout feeling we must of course set the fact that the pilgrim caravans were so notoriously riotous and debauched, that one of the first objects of the Wahabi reform was to cleanse them.

[2] Mill's *History*, p. 455. [3] Syed Ameer Ali, p. 184.

[4] Cf. Ewald's *Antiq. of Israel*, p. 367.

[5] See quotations in Reland, *De Rel. Moh.* p. 200. Cf. Morison's *Life of Bernard*, p. 374.

allowance of polygamy and divorce, the slavery and fatalism which prevail among Mohammedan populations.

That you may judge how far Mohammed is responsible for directing the hopes of his people to a material paradise, let me read you a fair specimen of the descriptions given in the Koran: "These are they who shall be brought nigh to God, in gardens of delight; a crowd from the ancients, and few from later generations. On inwrought couches reclining on them face to face: immortal youths go round about to them with goblets and ewers and a cup from a fountain; their brows ache not from it, nor fails the sense: and with such fruits as they shall make choice of, and with flesh of such birds as they shall long for, and theirs shall be the Houris with large dark eyes like close-kept pearls, a recompense for their labours past. No vain discourse shall they hear therein, nor charge of sin, but only the cry, Peace, peace! And the people of the right hand,—how happy the people of the right hand! amid thornless lote-trees and bananas clad with flowers, and extended shade and flowing waters and abundant fruits, unfailing and unforbidden, and lofty couches. Verily of a rare creation have we created the Houris, and we have made them ever virgins, dear to their spouses, of equal age with them, for the people of the right hand, a crowd from the ancients and a crowd from later generations."[1]

Such passages frequently occur in the earlier Suras of the Koran, and with little variation of phraseology; and I think a candid mind, accustomed to the Christian conception of heaven, must own to being somewhat shocked and disappointed by the low ideal of perfected human bliss set before the Mohammedan. One might suppose Mohammed had laid himself open to the insinuation conveyed in the well-known lines:

> "That prophet ill sustains his holy call,
> Who finds not heavens to suit the tastes of all;
> Houris for boys, omniscience for sages,
> And wings and glories for all ranks and ages."

Among Mohammedans there are many in every generation whose aspirations are spiritual, and who crave a heavenly life in which their purest and worthiest purposes shall not be defeated by the rebellings of their lower nature, nor even be delayed by providing for its necessities.[2] They, like the best among ourselves, seek not only an outwardly secure and

[1] Sura lvi. 10.

[2] Reland says, "Non igitur verum est, quod multi auctores qui oppugnarunt Mohammedanismum scripserunt, Muslimannos non alium beatitudinem in cœlo agnoscere, nisi usum voluptatum quæ sensus afficiunt" (p. 204).

affluent condition, but much more an inward resemblance to God Himself. It has therefore been commonly pleaded that these somewhat luscious descriptions in the Koran are to be understood as figurative, and to be interpreted as Christians interpret the pictures given in the Book of Revelation.[1] But there is a very conspicuous difference between the two cases. In the Book of Revelation, as in the other parts of Scripture, there is so much said of the spiritual joys of the future life, as to eclipse all that is said of pleasures of a lower kind, and to suggest to every reader a spiritual interpretation, even of the passages in which material descriptions are given; whereas in the Koran it must be owned that the promises of physical pleasure are, to say the least, very greatly in excess of promises of a higher kind. It will also be remarked that even where physical descriptions are used in the New Testament, they are never of the grosser kind. To the Christian conception, heaven is formed by the circumstance that it is the life suited to Jesus Christ glorified. We know what He found pleasure in on earth, and we conceive what are His heavenly joys. This defines heaven for us, and absolutely excludes from it everything gross,

[1] Lane, *Modern Egypt.* i. p. 84. Syed Ali's *Critical Exam.* pp. 277–285.

5

mean, and earthly. The Mohammedan has nothing so clear to rule his conceptions of the future life. Tradition indeed ascribes to Mohammed the saying that "the most favoured of God will be he who shall see his Lord's face night and morning—a felicity which will surpass all the pleasures of the body, as the ocean surpasses a drop of sweat." But in the Koran itself there is too little evidence that the habitual idea of heaven Mohammed himself possessed was other than that of an abode of peace, security, luxury, and reward.[1]

A deeper and more radical fault of Mohammedanism is the constancy and urgency of its appeal to the desire of reward. It has caught the primitive tone of the Mosaic legislation, and has altogether failed to correct this by introducing such motives as form the strength of the Christian character. It is true that to awaken in men a regard to the future is a feat worthy of the greatest moral teacher.[2] It furnishes him with a hold over the conduct of his disciples which is both justifiable and influen-

[1] Major Osborn has very distinctly illustrated the thoroughly materialistic character of Mohammed's conceptions. See *Islam under the Arabs*, pp. 34-38.

[2] "L'idée de l'avenir est une des plus puissantes en morale, et il est glorieux pour Mohammed de l'avoir mise en activité avec plus de force qu'aucun autre legislateur." Oelsner, *Des Effets*, p. 34.

tial. But a character formed chiefly on such a basis will inevitably lack the highest qualities.

> "Is selfishness
> For time, a sin—spun out to eternity,
> Celestial prudence? Shame!"

The hope of reward and the fear of punishment are rightly used until the inward disposition for virtue grows; but the religion in which these are the chief or the only motives brands itself as fit only for the lower strata of humanity and its undeveloped races. These motives are retained in Christianity, because Christianity appeals to the most degenerate as well as to the most mature and noble specimens of our race,[1] but it relies upon them only for pædagogic and occasional assistance, and looks to very different and much loftier motives for producing its highest strain of saintly character and of heroic virtue. And if, even with its mingling of higher motives, Christianity has suffered from the natural incapacity of men to live by them, and from their ineradicable disposition to barter with God, it is not surprising that a proud and self-righteous belief in the meritoriousness of good works has always been part and parcel of Mohammedanism, nor that

[1] "La seule religion chrétienne est proportionnée à tous, étant mêlée d'exterieur et d'interieur."—Pascal, *Pensées*, II. iv. 3.

it encourages the endeavour "to make one's soul" by fastings, alms, and endowments.[1]

As to the supposed fatalism of Islam, it is true that among Mohammedan populations there is a tendency to accept as destiny ills which might possibly be removed by vigorous action. "The great bulk of the people are passive: wars and revolutions rage around them: they accept them as the decrees of a fate it is useless to strive against." Such is the testimony of those who have lived for some time among Mohammedans.[2] This however seems more a matter of race than of religion, of individual temperament than of creed. The Arabs despise and reproach the Turks for their stupid apathy in ascribing to God what is the result of their own folly. "He bared his back," they say, "to the stings of the mosquitoes, and then cried out, God has decreed I should be stung."[3] It was an Arab who, when his religion was charged with fatalism, retorted, "Oh, man, if the wall against which I am now sitting were to shake above my head, should I fold my feet under me and say, 'Allah kereem' [It is the will of God], or should I use the legs God has given me to escape from it?"[4] Mo-

[1] Lady Duff Gordon's *Letters*.

[2] Osborn's *Islam under the Arabs*, p. 27.

[3] Burckhardt's *Notes*, i. 247.

[4] Lady Duff Gordon's *Last Letters*, p. 23.

hammed himself was as thorough a predestinarian as Calvin, but just as little of a fatalist. His belief in the decrees of God led him to accept the inevitable with resignation, but never interfered with his freedom and vigour of action. Again and again in the Koran he asserts that "God misleadeth whom He will, and whom He will He guideth,"[1] reproducing with almost verbal exactness the words of Paul. In accepting this doctrine he merely coincided, as Voltaire with his usual insight and knowledge has shown, with the almost universal opinion of antiquity. His followers have certainly in many instances perverted his doctrine, refusing to attempt the conversion of unbelievers on the ground that the number of the faithful is decreed, and cannot be increased or diminished;[2] and being unnerved in epidemics by the idea that their fate is unavoidable. And there are many sects among the Mohammedans, such as the Djabaris, the Rayatis, and the Djamis, who deny free-will altogether, as there are others who deny that Allah has predestined the deeds and inclinations of His creatures; but with neither of these deductions from his doctrine is Mohammed fairly chargeable.[3] He made no

[1] Sura xiv. 4. See also xiii. 30; iii. 139; viii. 17, &c.

[2] Lane, i. 353.

[3] Gobineau, *Des Religions*, &c., p. 72. Bosworth Smith's *Moham.* p. 191.

attempt to reconcile man's freedom of action with the predestination and overruling providence of God. He gave the freest play to both beliefs, and while he nerved his troops for battle by assuring them they could no more escape their fate at home than on the field, he forbade them to enter infected cities, and dealt with them as free agents. And probably his immediate followers, who had been brought up to believe that their fate was ruled by the stars, and fixed from the hour of their birth, felt that the doctrine of Mohammed was at once more rational and more encouraging.[1]

The effects upon society of the Christian and Mohammedan religions are most obviously distinguished by the position assigned to woman. Christian society is monogamist, Mohammedan polygamist. The law laid down in the Koran for the regulation of marriages is as follows: (Sura iv.) "Take in marriage, of the women who please you, two, or three, or four; but if ye fear that ye cannot act equitably to so many, take one only, or the slaves whom ye have acquired." In the opening words of the Sura from which this law is taken, there is, indeed, some slight indication of a leaning towards monogamy. "O men, fear the Lord, who hath created you out

[1] Philippsohn (*Develop. of Religious Idea*, p. 177) traces Mohammed's predestinarian belief to Sabeanism.

of one man, and out of him created his wife, and *from them two* hath multiplied many men and women; and fear God, by whom ye beseech one another; and respect women[1] who have borne you, for God is watching over you." Mohammedans, then, are, by the law of their prophet, allowed to possess four wives at the same time.[2]

The defence of polygamy has been undertaken from various points of view, and with varying degrees of insight and of earnestness. But one cannot detect much progress among its defenders. F. W. Newman has nothing to say in its favour which had not previously been suggested by Voltaire; nothing, we may say, which does not occur to any one who wishes to present the argument for a plurality of wives. It is somewhat late in the day to be called upon to argue for monogamy as abstractly right. Speculators like Aristotle,[3] who have viewed the subject both as statesmen having a regard to what is practicable and will conduce to social prosperity, and as philosophers reasoning from

[1] Lit. "the wombs."

[2] "Notwithstanding what Sale and some other learned men have asserted on this subject, the Muslim law certainly does not limit the number of concubine-slaves whom a man may have, whether in addition to, or without, a wife or wives."—Lane's *Mod. Egyptians*, i. 123; cf. Sale's *Koran*, Introd. sec. vi.

[3] Arist. *Econ.* i. 2, 8.

first principles, have long ago demanded for their ideal society not only monogamy, but also that mutual respect and love, and that strict purity and modesty, which polygamy kills. Let us say briefly that the only ground conscience recognises as warranting two persons to become one in flesh is, that they be first of all one in spirit. That absolute surrender of the person which constitutes marriage is justified only by the circumstance that it is a surrender of the heart as well, and that it is mutual. To an ideal love polygamy is abhorrent and impossible. As Mohammed himself, in another connection, and with more than his usual profundity, said, "God has not put two hearts in you." This is the grand law imbedded in our nature, and by which it is secured that the children born into the world be the fruit of the devoted surrender of one human spirit to another; by which—in other words—it is secured that love, the root principle of all human virtue and duty, be transmitted to the child and born in it. This is the beneficent law expressed in monogamy, and this law is traversed and robbed of its effects precisely in so far as even monogamous marriages are prompted by fleshly or worldly rather than by spiritual motives. The utilitarian argument Mr. Lecky[1] has summed up in three sentences:

[1] *Hist. of Europ. Morals*, ii. 295.

"Nature, by making the number of males and females nearly equal, indicates it as natural. In no other form of marriage can the government of the family, which is one of the chief ends of marriage, be so happily sustained;[1] and in no other does woman assume the position of the equal of man."

But we have here to do only with Mohammedan apologists, and their reasonings are somewhat perplexing; for they first maintain that nature intended us to be polygamists,[2] and then secondly declare that "the greatest and most reprehensible mistake committed by Christian writers is to suppose that Mohammed either adopted or legalised polygamy." Probably the most that can be said for Mohammed in regard to this matter is that he restricted polygamy, and that its abolition was impossible and unsuitable to the population he had to do with.

The allegation, however, that Mohammed confined polygamy within narrower limits than

[1] That Mohammedans are not unconscious of the disadvantage of polygamy, is shown by the Turkish proverb:

Duo asini, una Carawana:
Duæ uxores, unum forum.

As Pfeiffer (p. 424) explains it, "Duo asini tantum creant molestiæ quantum totus comitatus: et ubi duæ mulieres, ibi ob lites perpetuum est forum."

[2] Syed Ahmed's *Essay*, p. 8; and Syed Ameer Ali's *Crit. Exam.*, p. 226.

the Arabs had previously recognised, though true, is immaterial. For, in the first place, he restricted polygamy indeed in others, but not in his own case; and thus left upon the minds of his followers the inevitable impression that an unrestricted polygamy was the higher state of the two. In the second place, while he restricted the number of lawful wives, he did not restrict the number of slave-concubines. In the third place, his restriction was practically of little value, because very few men could afford to keep more than four wives. And, lastly, as to the principle, he left it precisely where it was, for as Mr. Freeman justly observes: "This is one of the cases in which the first step is everything. The difference between one wife and two is everything; that between four and five thousand is comparatively nothing."[1]

And if the principle be defended as at least relatively good, nothing is to be urged against this as matter of fact; although the circumstance has been overlooked, that already very many thousands of Christian Arabs had found it quite possible to live in monogamy. But that polygamy is not incompatible with a sound, if not perfectly developed, morality, and with the highest tone of feeling, no one who has read

[1] *Lectures*, p. 69.

the history of Israel will be disposed to deny. That it may suit a race in a certain stage of its development, and may in that stage lead to purer living and surer moral growth than its prohibition would, may be granted. But necessarily the religion which incorporates in its code of morals such allowances, stamps itself as something short of the final religion.

But the allowance of polygamy is by no means so destructive of social progress as the facility of divorce allowed by Mohammedan law. Syed Ameer Ali informs us that in India "ninety-five Moslems out of every hundred are perfect monogamists;" that "plurality of wives has come to be regarded as an evil, and as something opposed to the teaching of the Prophet;"[1] but the principle of monogamy requires, not only that a man should have but one wife at a time, but that marriage be indissoluble save by death or infidelity. It is nothing to the purpose to aver that such and such a proportion of Mohammedans have actually only one wife, if their law allows them to change that wife as often as they please; and if, in point of fact, they largely avail themselves of that liberty. Lane tells us that polygamy is exceptional in Egypt, but he adds that "there are certainly not many persons in Cairo who have not di-

[1] Syed Ali's *Crit. Exam.* pp. 227 and 246.

vorced one wife if they have been long married," and that there are many who in the course of ten years have married as many as twenty, thirty, or more wives."[1] No doubt this is not considered respectable, and no honourable man would so indulge his caprice; but, unfortunately, the law is made, not for the honourable, but for the dishonourable, and the law allows divorce on the easiest of terms. It is a principle of Mohammedan law that "a husband may divorce his wife without any misbehaviour on her part, or without assigning any cause."[2] The husband has only to say, "I divorce thee," or "thou art divorced;"[3] and without any legal procedure or appearance in a court of law, the wife is no longer a wife; whereas the woman can only divorce her husband before a court of law, and by proving ill-treatment or other reasonable ground.

Mohammed himself probably intended to improve the position of women. Possibly, like Milton, he doubted not "but with one gentle stroking to wipe away ten thousand tears out

[1] Lane's *Modern Egypt.* i. 227, 231. Burckhardt (*Notes on Bedouins*, i. 110) says: "Most Arabs are contented with a single wife, but for this monogamy they make amends by indulging in variety."

[2] *Tagore Law Lectures* for 1873, p. 389.

[3] Or any one of twenty other expressions which may be found in the Hidaya, or in the Tagore *Law Lectures.*

of the life of man." There is no reason to disbelieve the traditions which represent him as expressing indignation at men who dismissed their wives for slight offences. He himself, although on one occasion he might almost have been expected to use his legal right of divorce, did not do so. And there is a look of genuineness about the saying attributed to him: "God has not created anything on earth which He likes better than the emancipating of slaves, nor has He created anything which He dislikes more than divorce."[1] And in accordance with this feeling he did lay on the license of his followers certain restrictions, which have, however, proved altogether insufficient to make the law anything else than a mere abomination. The first restriction was to the effect that divorce was revocable until it had been pronounced three times. "Three successive declarations at a month's interval were necessary

[1] Quoted from the Mishkat by Syed Ali, p. 239. Syed Ahmed (p. 14 of Essay on question whether Islam has been beneficial) says: "Our Prophet constantly pointed out to his followers how opposed divorce was to the best interests of society; he always expatiated on the evils which flowed from it, and ever exhorted his disciples to treat women with respect and kindness, and to bear patiently their violence and ill-temper; and he always spoke of those who availed themselves of divorce in a severe and disparaging manner."

in order to make it irrevocable."[1] This was intended to protect women, not to say the husbands themselves, against the consequences of an ill-considered, passionate utterance of the fatal words. But it is notorious that all the benefit of this restriction is cancelled by Mohammedan law, which considers that the treble divorce uttered in one breath is as irrevocable as when it is uttered at three distinct times.[2] The second feature of the law of divorce which is claimed by Mohammedan apologists as a restriction, is the provision that when a woman has been irrevocably divorced she cannot ever be taken back by her husband, unless in the meantime she has been married to another man. The Mosaic law pronounced this to be "abomination before the Lord."[3] And it is possible that Mohammed, knowing how abhorrent it is to the Oriental that his wife be even seen by another man, considered that by issuing this enactment he was availing himself of the strongest possible deterrent from divorce. If so, he miscalculated the effect of his law, which has in point of fact degraded Moslem women to a deplorable extent.[4] The third restriction is

[1] Sedillot, quoted by Syed Ali; see also Mill's *History of Muhammedanism*, p. 341.

[2] See the Hidayah or Tagore *Law Lectures* as above.

[3] Deut. xxiv. 24.

[4] See Lane's *Modern Egypt.* i. 230; and the Arabic

the provision that when a husband divorces his wife he shall pay her dowry. And this is said to exercise some restraint upon the Turks, for though the minimum dowry recognised by law is only ten dirhems, or a few shillings, it is in some instances very large.[1]

The law of our religion and of our land takes the highest possible ground in the matter of marriage. It proceeds upon the understanding that the indissoluble quality of marriage is that which best guarantees a perception of its responsibilities, and a calm and well-considered acceptance of them. It proceeds upon the principle that prevention is better than cure, and that it is a wiser and safer policy to beget within the minds of men a strong sense of the irrevocable nature of the act than to encourage them to inconsiderate recklessness by the prospect of an easy divorce. It quite understands that there are many unhappy marriages; it does not shut its eyes to the scandals that from time to time occupy public attention; it does not

proverb, "A thousand lovers rather than one Mostahel;" on which Burckhardt's brief note (*Proverbs*, p. 25) is a caution to all apologists for this ill-advised law.

[1] Mill (*History of Muhammedanism*, p. 469) speaks as if this had considerable practical results: but Hughes (*Notes on Muhammadanism*, p. 122) says: "The difficulty of restoring the dowry is avoided by compelling the poor woman, through harsh treatment, to sue for a divorce herself, as in this case she can claim nothing."

ignore the voluntary separations, the quarrels, the murders,[1] which prove that so long as those who enter into marriage are imperfect, marriage itself will not always be satisfactory; but it assumes that however great are the evils of indissolubility, the evils of facile divorce would be greater still. All that can be pleaded in favour of a relaxation of our marriage laws has been put most pathetically and in his unapproachable language by Milton; but it is somewhat unfair of Mohammedan apologists to appeal to him as if he were an advocate of anything like the facile divorce of their own law. Such a system as their law upholds has always been the accompaniment either of an undeveloped or of a decaying stage in a people's history. The evils it wrought in imperial Rome, when, according to Seneca, women reckoned their years rather by their husbands than by the consuls,[2] are well known. "We find," says Mr. Lecky, "Cicero repudiating his wife Terentia, because he desired a new dowry;

[1] See the terrible paragraph in Legouvé's *Histoire des Femmes*, p. 232: "Qui crée parmi le peuple tant de bigamies de fait? L'indissolubilité. Qui fait que trois ouvriers sur huit ont deux ménages? L'indissolubilité," &c.

[2] "When Michaud asked an aged Egyptian whether he remembered the campaign of Napoleon, he answered that he had his seventeenth wife at that time."—Arnold's *Islam*, p. 211.

Augustus compelling the husband of Livia to repudiate her that he might marry her himself; Cato ceding his wife, with the consent of her father, to his friend Hortensius, and resuming her after his death; Mæcenas continually changing his wife; Sempronius Sophus repudiating his wife, because she had once been to the public games without his knowledge; Paulus Æmilius taking the same step without assigning any reason, and defending himself by saying, 'My shoes are new and well-made, but no one knows where they pinch me.'"[1]

Manifestly, however, the position of Mohammedan women is the result of instincts or principles lying far deeper than the opinion or religion of Mohammed. It is the result of the Semitic idea of woman, that she is a "vessel," a mere utensil for man's service.[2] Accordingly, after all that has been written both in condemnation and defence of this law, no utterance seems to go so directly to the root of the whole matter as the judgment pronounced by the thoroughly informed and impartial Lane.[3] "The laws," he says, "relating to marriage and the license of polygamy, the facility of divorce allowed by the Koran, and the permission of

[1] Lecky's *European Morals*, ii. 324.

[2] Cf. Fairbairn's *Studies*, p. 279. [3] *Mod. Egyp.* i. 121.

concubinage, are essentially the natural and necessary consequences of the main principle of the constitution of Moslem society—the restriction of the intercourse of the sexes before marriage. Few men would marry if he who was disappointed in a wife whom he had never seen before were not allowed to take another; and in the case of a man's doing this, his own happiness, or that of the former wife, or the happiness of both these parties, may require his either retaining this wife or divorcing her."

Mohammed himself was a man of a compassionate and humane disposition, and there can, I think, be no doubt that he intended to ameliorate the condition of slaves. Had he conceived the idea of emancipating them, he would probably have found it an idea impossible to execute; and in declaring all Moslems brethren, he took the surest means in his power of eventually accomplishing this end, and in the meantime of securing their good treatment. His parting admonitions to his followers on this subject are too important to be omitted. "Your slaves!" he says, "see that ye feed them with such food as ye eat yourselves; and clothe them with the stuff ye wear; and if they commit a fault which ye are not inclined to forgive, then sell them, for they are the servants of the

Lord, and are not to be tormented. Ye people! hearken to my speech, and comprehend the same; know that every Moslem is the brother of every other Moslem; all of you are on the same equality; ye are one brotherhood."[1] And it must be owned that, at least in certain countries, the doctrine of human equality thus proclaimed has received practical exemplifications which are sadly wanting in the parallel region of Christian practice. The Caliph Omar, leading his camel while his slave rides; the prophet's daughter Fatimah, taking her turn at the mill with her own slaves; these are but specimens of the scrupulous observance in general paid by Moslems to the injunctions of their prophet. Unfortunately, whatever kindly intention Mohammed had towards the slave, and whatever beneficial results might have been wrought by his bold proclamation of the equality of all believers, have been frustrated by the Koran's sanction of concubinage. There is no disguising the fact that it is this allowance which maintains the slave-trade with all its well-known abominations and horrors. It is this system, distinctly sanctioned in the Koran, and practised by Mohammed himself, which is responsible for the degradation and misery which become the life-long lot of the wretched girls

[1] Muir, iv. 239.

who survive the terrible transit down the Nile under the tender mercies of the brutal Gelláb̦s.[1] Enlightened Mohammedans[2] themselves are humiliated by the pollutions and misery attaching to this system. They say in so many words that it is "to the lasting disgrace of the majority of the followers of Mohammed," that "slavery has been allowed to flourish by purchase and other means,"[3] and that the day is come for the Moslems to show "the falseness of the aspersions cast on the memory of the great and noble prophet, by proclaiming in explicit terms that slavery is reprobated by their Faith, and discountenanced by their Code." But while we honour the desire of these men to cleanse their religion of so black a stain, how are they to stir a single Mohammedan community to abolish an indulgence to which their "great and noble prophet" showed them the way, and which is regulated for in the Koran? Slavery can only be abolished when concubinage is abolished; and when concubinage is abolished, the whole character of Islam, and especially its attitude to its prophet and its sacred book, must be altered.

[1] Lane's *Mod. Egyp.* i. 236.

[2] Syed Ahmed, p. 25. [3] Syed Ali, p. 259.

II.

MOHAMMEDANISM:

ITS SUCCESS AND FAILURE.

"Be joyful, be joyful; my followers are like rain, of which it is unknown whether the first or last fall will be the best; or like a garden from which a multitude has been fed one year, and then another the next year, and perhaps the last is more numerous than the first, and better."—MOHAMMED.

II.

BEFORE the appearance of Mohammed, the highest and the lowest forms of religion existed side by side among the tribes of Arabia.[1] The original faith appears to have been the simple monotheism of Abraham. But a creed which had no elaborate symbolism, no ritual but that which inculcated prayer at sunrise, noon, and sunset, proved too spiritual for the wild and impressible Arabians. Praying *at* sunrise quickly became praying *to* sunrise; and the idea of an unseen God who ruled the heavens and guided them in their wanderings, was

[1] The great authority for the Pre-islamic condition of Arabia is still Pocock's "libellus incomparabilis," entitled, *Specimen Historiæ Arabum.* Oxon. 1650. (Notes dated 1648); of which Gibbon justly says, "Consult, peruse, and study the *Specimen.* The 358 notes [pages of notes?] form a classic and original work on the Arabian antiquities." Pocock makes it his business to explain "quales invenerit Arabes suos Mohammedes, et quales reliquerit." Rasmussen's *Historia Arabum ante Islamismum* and his *Additamenta* are also works of original research, and are well worth consulting.

obscured by their dependence on the motions of the planets for all their prognostications and reckonings. What their own life and habits chiefly impressed upon them was that everything depended on these inaccessible heavenly bodies; and so their worship gradually was directed to Sabaoth, the host of heaven, and they received the name of Sabians.[1] But at a later period, when Neo-Platonism was adopting and adapting every form of worship, it nowhere found a more promising field than in this worship of the heavens. For it was the favourite idea of this school, an idea countenanced by their Master, that the abyss existing between God and His creatures was bridged by intermediary gods. These intermediate gods were supposed to animate or have their residence in, or at least to make themselves visible and influential through, the planets. The planets therefore must be carefully observed; their risings, settings, conjunctions, and influences noted, and all human actions regulated in conformity with these. If Saturn be in the

[1] "Notum est Abrahamum patrem nostrum educatum esse in fide Zabaeorum, qui statuerunt nullum esse deum præter stellas" Maimonides, quoted in Wright's *Christianity in Arabia*, p. 27). The traditions regarding Abraham are given by Caussin de Perceval, i. 161; who also (i. 349) names the different planets worshipped by the various tribes.

ascendant, then it is advisable to select at that time such dresses, seals, amulets, incantations, and prayers as may be supposed pleasing to this planetary god. Another step in the downward process was taken, when permanent and stationary representations of these gods were felt to be superior to the planets themselves, which were sometimes out of sight when their help was required. Images were therefore formed, and worship was offered to them rather than to the stars they represented.[1]

It will thus be understood how a vague belief in a supreme God continued to underlie the profuse idolatry of the Arabian tribes. "I dedicate myself to Thy service, O God! I dedicate myself to Thy service, O God! Thou hast no companion, except him of whom Thou art absolute Master, and of whatever is his." This seems an explicit enough confession of monotheism. Yet in practice great deference was shown to these companions of God, though their powers were but delegated. Thus, if on offering their first-fruits some which belonged to God fell over to the idol's portion, they made no restitution. If while irrigating the idol's ground, the water ran over to God's land, they dammed it up; while if it ran from

[1] Pocock, *Specimen*, 138 *et seq.* :—An admirable account is given of *Zabism* in Chamber's Encyclopædia.

God's to the idol's, they did not interfere, conceiving that the Supreme was more placable than the inferior; and transferring, as Freeman remarks, their knowledge of earthly courts to that of heaven.[1] In the Kaabah itself, or conspicuous in its sacred enclosures, were no fewer than 360 idols, one for each day in the lunar year of Arabia. Chief among these was Hobal, the huge image of red agate, revered as the giver of rain, and holding in his hand the pointless and featherless arrows of divination. Here also—crowning proof of the comprehensiveness of the early religion—was, perhaps, or a painting of the Madonna and child.[2] But the idols against which the Koran inveighs, were the supposed antediluvian relics—Wadd, in the form of a man; Sawâ, represented as a woman; Yaghûth, worshipped in the shape of a lion; Yaük, who was known under the figure of a horse; and Nasr, under that of an eagle. Still more firmly rooted in the affections of the people, and more obnoxious to Mohammed, were the three goddesses Al-Lat, Al-Uzza, and

[1] See Sale's *Introduction*, and Freeman's *Lectures*, p. 30.

[2] Possibly writers have too easily assumed that the mother and child represented the Virgin and our Lord. In India, Devaki and Crishna are so represented; in Egypt, Isis and Horus; and in Greece, Venus and Cupid. See Rawlinson's *Herod.* ii. p. 539.

Manah.[1] "What think ye," he says, "of Al-Lat, and Al-Uzza, and Manah, that other third goddess? Have ye male children and God female? This is an unjust partition. They are no other than empty names, which ye and your fathers have named goddesses."[2] Or as another Sura more fully explains his meaning:[3] "They attribute daughters unto God; but unto themselves children of the sex they desire. When any of them is told that a female child is born to him, his face grows black, and he is deeply grieved; he hideth himself from the people, because of the ill tidings which have been told him; considering within himself whether he shall keep it with disgrace, or whether he shall bury it in the dust." Beneath this worship of stars, of the images of intermediate gods or illustrious ancestors, lay the deeper depth of Fetishism. As the straw is clutched by the drowning man, so, to those who had nothing else to trust in, a tree, or a stone, or even a lump of dough, was enough to admit of the expression of confidence. And it might be difficult to determine whether, when the Hanifites in time of famine ate their god, the ridicule of their enemies was excited more

[1] See Wilkinson's note on Alilat in Rawlinson's *Herod.* iii. 8. And for the sites of the temples of these goddesses, Caussin de Percival's *Histoire des Arabes*, i. 269.

[2] Sura liii. [3] Sura xvi.

by triumph over their helplessness or in satire of their superstition.[1]

As their notions of the divine government were confused and various, so also were their ideas of the future state. Some believed in an eternal order of nature, which admitted of no act of creation and of no final, designed consummation in which all beings who had consciously contributed to it would play a part. Some admitted a creative beginning of things, but could not believe in any final restoration. Some accepted both,[2] and in pursuance of their belief in a state after death tied a camel to the grave, that when the dead man rose he might not be exposed to the ignominy of walking on his own feet to the judgment-bar. Others again believed in metempsychosis, and adopted the curious semi-materialistic notion that out of the blood gathered about the brain of the dead, there was formed a bird, which they called Hamah, and which visited the sepulchre once in a hundred years.[3] If the dead man had

[1] Comederunt Hanifitæ dominum suum ob famem antiquam et inopiam." The saying of a Tamamite reported by Rasmussen, *Additamenta*, p. 76.

[2] Mosheim is of opinion that their ideas of immortality were derived from Jewish or Christian sources, but this seems very doubtful. See Mosheim's *Diss. ad Hist. Eccl.* ii. 648.

[3] Pocock, pp. 134, 5.

been murdered, his spirit having transmigrated into this bird, it hovered over his grave, crying, Oscuni, oscuni ! (give me drink, give me drink !) until the blood of the murderer was shed to satiate it.

In conjunction with such idolatries and superstitions, one expects to find a very imperfect civilization, and some habits and customs which may be termed barbarous. "An infinity of tribes, some settled, but the greater number nomadic, without community of interests or a common centre, ordinarily at war with one another—such," says one of our best authorities,[1] "was Arabia in the time of Mohammed." Tribal wars, family feuds, and marauding expeditions were so much the normal state of things, that it was only by agreeing to suspend hostilities during certain months of the year that the necessary pursuits could be followed with safety. The state of society must have resembled that of the ancient Germans, of whom Tacitus says, "pigrum et iners videtur sudore acquirere quod possis sanguine parare ;" or that significantly hinted at in the suggestive complaint of Wat Tinlinn—

> "They burned my little lonely tower :
> It had not been burnt this year and more !"

Their leisure seems to have been chiefly spent

[1] Dozy, *Histoire des Mussulmans*, i. 16.

in gambling and drinking. Only a small portion in some of the districts, and none at all in others, could read and write.[1] This inability to read made them prize highly recitations of poetry, whether original or not. These poems were their tribal and family archives, maintaining the memory of heroic deeds, and of ancient friendships and feuds. They were of course numerous; so much so, that some centuries after Mohammed, Hammad the narrator undertook to repeat one hundred pre-Mohammedan poems for every letter of the alphabet, and wore out the patience of his hearers before exhausting his stock.[2]

The ugliest features, however, of the times of ignorance, were the marriage laws and the custom of burying female children alive. It was customary for the son to inherit the father's wives along with his other property. Female infants have never been much in repute in barbarous countries. To this day the Breton farmer, to whom a daughter is born, says, "My wife has had a miscarriage."[3] In Sparta, of ten exposed children, seven were female. The Hebrew law reckoned a woman ceremonially

[1] Pocock's authorities (pp. 156, 7) imply even greater ignorance.

[2] Wright's *Early Christianity in Arabia*, p. 6.

[3] Legouvé, *Hist. des Femmes*, pp. 13–17.

unclean if she gave birth to a son, but doubly so if she gave birth to a daughter. But while those countries are the exceptions in which the custom of exposing children has not at some time being practised, it was practised in Arabia in a more than usually cold-blooded manner. Sometimes, indeed, the child was made away with as soon as born, but often she was allowed to attain her sixth year, and then, when she might be supposed to have wound herself inextricably round the affections of her parents, her father would one day say to his wife, "Perfume and adorn her, that I may take her away to her mothers." This being done, he would lead her to a pit he had prepared, bid her look into it, and, standing behind her, would push her in, and immediately fill it in level with the ground.[1] Some idea of the extent to which this was practised may be formed from the fact that one man had saved from this horrible inhumation no fewer than 280 girls.[2]

But Judaism and Christianity were also largely, if not very purely, represented in Arabia before the time of Mohammed. Even before the Christian era, the Jews had firmly established themselves in Arabia. And it is probable

[1] Pocock, p. 336.

[2] Rasmussen's *Additamenta ad Hist. Arabum ante Islam*, p. 67.

that their colonies already thriving in that mercantile country would offer considerable attractions to those who were forced to flee from their own land during and after the Roman invasion. Several of the tribes, notably those of Kendah and Kenanah, of Al Hareth Ibn Caab, and the powerful tribe of Hamyarites, professed the Jewish religion.[1] At one time they could raise an army of 120,000 men,[2] which, thanks to the unity maintained by their creed, was probably a larger army than any other community of Arabia could have brought into the field. "Centuries before Mohammed, Kheibar, five days from Medina, and Yemen in South Arabia, were in the hands of the Jews."[3] In Medina itself there was a large Jewish population, said to be descended from those who fled from Nebuchadnezzar, and their influence is clearly understood when we see the pains which the prophet took at the outset of his mission to conciliate them, and the difficulties he found in subduing them. In the rites of Islam—in circumcision, fasting, pilgrimage, the Kibleh in prayer—the family connection

[1] "Judaismo addicti erant Himyaritæ, Cananitæ, Gens Haretsi, filii Câbi, atque Cenditæ."—Rasmussen, *Additamenta*, p. 76. Pocock, *Specimen*, p. 136.

[2] Milman's *History of the Jews*, iii. p. 88.

[3] Deutsch's *Islam*, p. 90, and for details see Wright's *Christianity in Arabia*, p. 23.

between the sons of Ishmael and the Beni-Israel is discernible. And the popularity of the Jewish Haggadah and Halachah is witnessed in every legend of Islam and in every Sura of the Koran.[1]

As the Judaism prevalent in Arabia was rather of the Rabbinic than the pure Old Testament type, so the Christianity with which the tribes were acquainted was meagre, degenerate, apocryphal. It found some acceptance in the tribes of Rabia and Gassan, and a few bishoprics were established in friendly districts.[2] It is difficult, however, to estimate the value of this Christianity, or to determine whether it would have been a greater boon to Arabia than Mohammedanism. On the one hand we have the fact that at Nadjran about 20,000 Christians preferred a horrible death rather than abjuration of their religion. On the other hand we have the notoriously superficial character of the Arabs, coupled with the saying of Ali, regarding the tribe in which Christianity had found its heartiest welcome. "The Taghlib," he said, "are not Christians; they have borrowed from Christianity only the custom of drinking wine."[3] It

[1] Deutsch's *Islam*, p. 90. See also Rodwell's *Koran*, passim.

[2] See Caussin de Perceval's *Histoire*, i. 348; and Pocock, p. 136.

[3] Dozy's *Histoire*, i. 20.

is not likely that a religion so uncongenial to the Arab character would have made much more way than it had done in previous centuries. And although we find the Christian King Abrahah leading 60,000 men in a crusade against Mecca, we cannot conclude that these were all Christians. We know, indeed, that they were not. The only inferences we can safely draw are that at this date—the year of Mohammed's birth and of the destruction of Abrahah's army — Christianity was an important factor in Arabian society, and that had this crusade been successful, it might have become the dominant religion.[1]

But it was not only Christianity that failed to gain any firm anchorage in the Arab character, their ancestral religions were held with little greater tenacity. They were radically irreligious, capable of adhering to forms of worship even while reverence was entirely awanting. The story of Amrolcais is typical and significant. Setting out to avenge his father's murder, he entered the temple of the idol Dhou-'l-Kholosa to consult the oracle by means of the usual three arrows, inscribed respectively, *Permission*, *Prohibition*, *Delay*. Having drawn *Prohibition*, he tried again. But three times over he drew

[1] See Wright's *Christianity in Arabia;* Gagnier's *Vie de Mahomet*, i. 70–75. Freeman's *Lectures*, p. 34.

the same arrow, forbidding his enterprise. Breaking the arrows, and hurling the fragments at the idol's head, he cried, "Wretch! had it been thy father who had been killed, you would not have prohibited revenge."[1] It was certainly no hopeful task which Mohammed undertook when he proposed by the influence of religion to combine into one nation tribes so incapable of being deeply influenced by any religion,[2] and so irreconcilably opposed to one another; to abolish customs which had the sanction of immemorial usage; and to root out an idolatry, which, if it had no profound hold upon the spiritual nature, was at least bound up with old family traditions and well-understood tribal interests.

But if the difficulties of the task were sufficiently apparent, there were also circumstances which made it at least possible. Chief among these was the existence of a small number of persons amcng whom a spirit of religious inquiry was cultivated. Not only had there been from time to time men of devout feeling and high moral tone, such as Hinzilah, Khalid, Asad Ibn Karb, and Abdolmottaleb himself,[3]

[1] Dozy, i. 22.

[2] "Il lui fallait transformer, metamorphoser, une nation sensuelle, sceptique et railleuse."—Dozy, i. 24.

[3] See the account of his Abrahamic surrender of his best loved son, in Caussin de Perceval, i. 264.

all of whom had attempted reforms with more or less success; but there were also men known as Hanyfs, or Puritans,[1] who distinctly renounced the idolatrous practices of their countrymen, and set themselves to seek the pure religion of Abraham.

It is related of four of these Hanyfs, that during one of the religious festivals of Mecca, they held aloof and conversed with one another in some such terms as these: "Our tribesmen are in error: they have destroyed religion. Are we to encompass a stone which neither hears nor sees, and which neither hurts nor helps us? Let us seek a better faith." Whereupon they abandoned their homes and journeyed in foreign lands, seeking the Hanyfite faith, that is, the religion of Abraham.[2] These four men were Waraka, Othman, Obaydallah, and Zaid. Of these, the first two were cousins of Khadijah, Mohammed's first wife, and in frequent intercourse with him; the third was his own cousin; and all three found their way to Christianity.

[1] *Pervert*, or *convert*. See Rodwell's *Koran*, p. 216. Sprenger (i. 67) says it originally meant one who does not believe in the true religion, but it is used in the Koran of those who abjured the popular religions and became Moslems. Thus *Freethinker*, *Pervert*, or *Purist*, may all translate the word according to the point of view of the translator.

[2] Sprenger, i. 81, and Caussin de Perceval, i. 321.

With Zaid the search for truth was more perplexed and less satisfactory in its results. Even as an old man he was seen leaning his back against the Kaabah, vehemently repudiating the idolatrous worship going on around him, and yet sadly stretching his hands upwards with the yearning prayer of the baffled yet whole-hearted man: "O God, if I knew what form of worship is the most pleasing to Thee, so would I serve Thee; but I know it not." In all his travels he had found nothing which gave the light he sought; and, excluded from his town by those who would not have a censor so keen and bold, he lived his remaining days and died on the neighbouring hill Hira; and doubtless Mohammed was essentially right in saying, "I will pray for him: in the Resurrection he too will gather a Church around him."

Men such as these could not but vastly quicken and deepen the thoughts of Mohammed. It was to this little body of seekers for the truth he belonged. He called himself a Hanyf, and during the first period of his prophetic office he aimed at nothing else than to restore the religion of Abraham, the Hanyfite creed.[1] So in one of the most important Suras of the Koran

[1] "Er nennt sich selbst einen Hanyf, und während der ersten Periode seines Lehramtes hat er wenig anderes gethan als ihre Lehre bestätigt."—Sprenger's *Muh.* p. 45.

he says: "Abraham, the founder of Hanyfism, was in fact neither Jew nor Christian, but a Hanyf and a Moslim, and not an Idolater." And whether he intended it designedly, or was unconsciously led, it was of immense importance that he did hit upon Abraham as the founder of his religion. For amidst all the feuds and enmities, the variances and irreconcilable ideas and practices of Jews, Christians, and idolaters, there was but this one point in common, their reverence for Abraham. The Jews at first seem to have expected that Mohammed would be little else than a champion of Judaism in a slightly modified form. The Hanyfs, and even the idolaters, would gather round a man who merely proclaimed a return to the religion of their fathers. And the Christians, though they might have their fears, would congratulate themselves that here at least was a practical religion and not another obscure and misty heresy. And, above all, let us take note that the society in which such men as these Hanyfs could be produced must have been one in which there was some religious stir and preparedness for any definite and resolute teaching.

But without Mohammed himself, without that peculiar force and quality which he and no other man brought to these circumstances, Islam would never have existed. The Arabian mind was prepared, and the state of the world gave opportunity for a new power to find play in it, but this preparedness and opportunity none but Mohammed knew how to use. When the irresistible Amru visited Omar at Medina, the caliph expressed a wish to see the sword which had slain so many of the enemies of the faith. Amru drew a short and ordinary scimitar, and, perceiving the surprise of the caliph, said, "Alas! the sword itself, without the arm of the master, is no sharper nor heavier than the sword of Farezdak the poet." And similarly we may say that without the mind of Mohammed there was no more material for founding a new religion, no state of matters more suggestive of world-wide conquest in that generation than in any other. The strong arm avails little without its suitable weapon, but the weapon is still more vain without the skilful and untiring arm. But for the concurrence of circumstances the greatest religious leaders might have died without a follower or a convert;[1] yet circumstances need their great man quite as much as the great man needs favouring circumstances. We must know the man if we would understand his religion and the causes of its success.

Tradition provides us with ample materials

[1] Jowett's *Epistles of Paul*, i. 356.

for seeing the man as he appeared to his contemporaries. Thoroughly incongruous with the substantial nature of his work, and the solid place it has in the world's history, are the fantastic details indulged in by some of his early biographers; such as that his body cast no shadow, that his spittle sweetened salt water, and that he seemed to tower above all those who approached him, a tradition which may have arisen from the magnificent poise of his head. He himself rather encouraged the belief in the "seal of prophecy"—a mark between his shoulders, on which were inscribed the words, "God is alone, without companions." But eliminating what has obviously no foundation, much remains to depict the man as he was. Like some other great men, he was scarcely above the middle height, but of dignified and commanding appearance. An admiring follower says of him, "He was the handsomest and bravest, the brightest-faced and most generous of men." He had the broad chest and firmly-knit limbs of the man of action, the large well-shaped head of the man of thought and capacity, the fine, long, arching eyebrows [1] and brilliant

[1] "Les sourcils longs et déliés qui s'approchaient mutuellement, sans néanmoins se toucher, et se confondre tout à fait."—Gagnier, *Vie de Mahomet*, ii. 313, where the fullest description of the prophet's appearance, disposi-

black eyes which sometimes betoken genius and always betoken an emotional nature. His mouth was large but well formed, a kindly and eloquent mouth, with teeth "like hailstones," in Arab phraseology; that is, we presume, white and glittering, so as to excuse his favourite and almost constant use of a toothpick. The large blood-vessel in his brow filled and darkened and throbbed when he was angry, which, if it proves him to have been of an excitable temperament, illustrates also the self-control which enabled him habitually to command the storm within. It was in public speaking that the fiery and vehement nature of the man was allowed to appear. "In ordinary address, his speech was slow, distinct, and emphatic; but when he preached, his eye would redden, his voice rise high and loud, and his whole frame become agitated with passion, even as if he were warning the people of an enemy about to fall on them the next morning or that very night."[1] His gait was as expressive as his appearance. His step is described as resembling that of a man descending a hill, and he walked with such extreme rapidity that those who accompanied him were kept at a half run. This swift

tion, and habits, is given. The picture given in Deutsch's *Islam* (pp. 71–73) is one of the finest specimens of his great literary skill.

[1] Muir, iv. 316.

and decided walk seems eminently characteristic. It was that of a man who knew where he was going, and meant that nothing should prevent him being there.

His manner was that of the perfect Arab gentleman, who knows no distinction of ranks, and is as courteous and formally polite to rags as to purple. He was gracious, unassuming, most patient and kindly to his slaves, adored by his followers, captivating to strangers. He was the most accessible of men: to adopt the expressive simile used by his admirers, "open as the river's bank to him that draweth water therefrom."[1] An unusually delicate consideration for the feelings and comfort of those about him betrayed itself in his whole manner. He found it almost impossible to say "No" to any petitioner, and he never declined the invitation or small offering even of the meanest of the people. He understood both joy and sorrow, and—conclusive proof of his wide and genuine humanity—had an equally ready sympathy for both. With all reverence we may say, He was among men as he that serveth.[2] In the last years of his life, when his strength was failing, his uncle Abbas proposed that he should occupy

[1] Weil, p. 347. Muir, iv. 304.

[2] "Il servait volontiers ceux qui le servaient."—Gagnier, ii. 320.

an elevated seat in the mosque, that the people might not throng him. "No," said Mohammed, "surely, I will not cease from being in the midst of them, dragging my mantle behind me thus, and covered with their dust, until that the Lord give me rest from among them."[1] He had no kindred with the species of great man who gives you two fingers and the head of a walking-stick to shake; but when any one addressed him he turned full round and gave to them the attention, not only of a glance or of the ear, but of the full countenance. In greeting any one he was never the first to withdraw his hand. Habitually taciturn, he was yet delightful in his hours of relaxation;

> "Exceeding wise, fair-spoken, and persuading;
> Lofty and sour to those that loved him not,
> But to those men that sought him, sweet as summer."

"Ten years," said Anas, his servant, "have I been about the prophet, and he never said as much as 'uff' to me." He was fond of children, having a kind word for those he saw in the street, and not ashamed to be seen, by astounded Arab chiefs, carrying and fondling one of his own little girls. Indeed, there is no incident in the life of Mohammed so affecting, nor any in which we are more drawn

[1] Muir, iv. 255.

to love the man, than that of the death of his infant child Ibrahim. It is with pure compassion we are spectators of the bitter grief and uncontrollable sobbings of the strong man, and hear at last, as he puts the little body back into the nurse's arms, his simple, pious lamentation, "Ibrahim, O Ibrahim! if it were not that the promise is faithful, and the hope of resurrection sure—if it were not that this is the way to be trodden by all, and the last of us shall join the first—I would grieve for thee with a grief deeper even than this."[1]

Carlyle, amending Shakespere, assures us that "the man who cannot laugh is not only fit for treasons, stratagems, and spoils; but his whole life is already a treason and a stratagem." Mohammed stands this test well. There was nothing guarded nor constrained in the uncontrollable fits of laughter with which he treated the drolleries of his child-wife Ayesha;[2] nothing pompous in the hearty naturalness with which he entered into her games, ran races with her, or told her amusing stories.[3] And yet, with all this fund of playfulness, it is this same Ayesha who tells us that he was "bashful as a virgin behind her veil." The blemishes in his character are indeed sufficiently obvious, but they are

[1] Muir, iv. 165. [2] Weil, p. 88.
[3] Sprenger iii. 62.

those of his race. He was not above availing himself of the dagger of the professional assassin to remove a dangerous enemy. He used the customary treacheries of Arab warfare. He could even stoop so low as to furnish an officer of his own with ambiguous instructions, carefully screening himself from the infamy and danger of an unjustifiable raid, while he hoped to enjoy the advantages derived from it. But we are to remember the axiom of Captain Burton, that "lying is to the Oriental meat and drink and the roof that covers him."[1] His courage is not wholly above suspicion;[2] on the field of battle he almost never played a conspicuous part, and, like Napoleon, was always provided with the means of securing his own safety by swift retreat. But he had also the Napoleonic power of discerning and winning to himself the foremost of his contemporaries, and of inspiring one and all of his followers with enthusiastic ardour in his cause. Of an intensely nervous organization, he was very sensitive to praise and blame. The satirical poets who lampooned him he found it much more difficult to forgive than if they had opposed him merely with the sword.

His style of living was simple even for an Arab. "The true Bedouin," says Burton, "is

[1] Burton's *Pilgrimage*, iii. 294.

[2] Weil, 344. Muir, iv. 313–14.

an abstemious man, capable of living for six months on ten ounces of food a day. The milk of a single camel, and a handful of dates dry, or fried in clarified butter, suffices for his wants."[1] According to the testimony of Ayesha, "months used to pass and no fire would be lighted in Mohammed's house, either for baking bread or cooking meat." "How then did ye live?" asked some one of her. "By the two black things, dates and water, and such of the citizens as had milch cattle would send us a little milk—the Lord requite them! The prophet never enjoyed the luxury of two kinds of food the same day; if he had flesh, there was nothing else; and so if he had dates; so likewise if he had bread."[2] On his death-bed his wife had to borrow oil for the lamp. And when he learned on the same occasion that there was a small sum of money in the house, he ordered it to be divided among certain indigent families, and then lying back, said, "Now I am at peace. Verily it would not have become me to meet my

[1] Lady Duff Gordon records the exclamation of an Effendi on hearing how Europeans live. "It is the will of God; but it must be a dreadful fatigue to them to eat their dinner."—*Last Letters*, p. 85. "An Arab will live for months together upon the smallest allowance; and then, if an opportunity should offer, he will devour at one sitting the flesh of half a lamb without any injury to his health." —Burckhardt, *Notes on Bedouins*, i. 242.

[2] Muir, iv. 329.

Lord, and this gold in my possession."[1] He did not like another to do for him anything he could do for himself. He might be seen patching his own clothes, cobbling his own sandals, milking the goats, helping in the house work, or carrying a basket from the market.[2] To the last he retained the simple habits of his youth. His establishment was of the plainest description, and was for a while retained after his death to rebuke the growing luxury of the Moslems. It consisted of nine small huts which a tall man could see over, four built of unbaked bricks and five of palm branches, with curtains of leather or hair-cloth for doors. To each of his wives one of these was allotted, he himself living in one or another of them.[3] His bed was a mat coarsely plaited with ropes of palm-fibre, which left its marks on his side when he rose. Abdallah, his servant, seeing this, rubbed the place and said, "Let me, I pray thee, spread a soft covering for thee over this mat." "Not so," replied Mohammed. "What have I to do

[1] Muir, iv. 273. [2] Weil, p. 343.

[3] "The house of Haritha was next to that of Mahomet. Now, whenever Mahomet took to himself another wife, he added a new house to the row, and Haritha was obliged successively to remove his house and build on the space beyond. At last this was repeated so often that the prophet said to those about him, 'Verily it shameth me to turn Haritha over and over again out of his house.'" Tradition in Muir, iv. 337.

with the comforts of this life? The world and I, what connection is there between us? Verily, the world is no otherwise than as a tree unto me; when the traveller hath rested under its shade, he passeth on."[1] His one luxury was perfumes. "The prophet," says Ayesha, "loved three things—women, scents, and food: he had his heart's desire of the two first, but not of the last."

Add to this that which made all his other qualities tell, his unconquerable determination. He was indomitable. The Arabs have a proverb about the man that finds good in evil: "Throw him into the river, and he will rise with a fish in his mouth." Mohammed was such a man; finding his opportunity in the most unfavourable circumstances, hopeful and sanguine in a quite extraordinary degree. When he and Abu Bekr were lying concealed in a cave, and heard the angry voices of their pursuers coming closer and closer, his brave and steadfast companion whispered, "What shall we do? We are but two against so many." Mohammed whispered back, "Not so, we are three; God is with us."

Such a man was born to greatness. A man so unlike other men, and yet so interested in

[1] Muir, iii. 297.

them—dreamy with the dreaminess of genius, and yet eminently capable and prompt in all practical matters, sympathetic and commanding—he was bound to move his generation deeply. And undoubtedly it was largely to his personal influence with men, and the impression his character made upon them, that his religion owed its success. It was those who knew him best and were most constantly with him who first attached themselves to his cause.

The idea that the success of Islam was due to the sensual inducements it proposed to its adherents was exploded by Voltaire. To the canons, monks, and curates who thus calumniated Mohammedanism, he addressed the pertinent question: "Were there imposed upon you a law that you should neither eat nor drink from four in the morning till ten at night through the whole month of July; that you should abstain from wine and gaming under penalty of damnation; that you should make a pilgrimage across burning deserts; that you should bestow at least 2½ per cent. of your revenue on the poor; and that, having been accustomed to eighteen wives, you should suddenly be limited to four,—would you call this a sensual religion?"[1] As compared with the previous

[1] *Dict. Phil.* s.v. Mahométans.

habits of the people to whom it was proposed, Mohammedanism had not any sensual attractions to present; and if it had possessed such, these would not account for its success. "A motive of sensuality could never of itself make the fortune of a religion."[1] But this motive, indirectly and in combination with others, did operate for the advancement of Islam. The soldiers of the Crescent were not primed for battle by doses of arrack and brandy; but intoxication of another kind drove them to deeds of impetuous and reckless valour. "I see," cried Khaled's youthful cousin at the battle of Emesa, "I see the black-eyed houris of Paradise. One of them, if seen on earth, would make mankind die of love. They are smiling on us. One of them waves a handkerchief of green silk and holds a cup of precious stones. She beckons me. Come hither quickly, she cries, my well-beloved."[2]

For unquestionably the grand cause of the success of Islam was its use of the sword, its amalgamation of propagandism with territorial conquest. The apparent profundity of the well-

[1] "Un motif de sensualité ne sauroit jamais à lui seul faire la fortune d'une religion."—Oelsner, *Des Effets*, &c., p. 18.

[2] Irving, *Successors of Mahomet*, p. 67, and Gibbon, cap. li.

known dictum of Carlyle turns out, when you examine it, to be mere sophistication. "The sword indeed," he says, "but where will you get your sword? Every new opinion, at its starting, is precisely in a minority of one. In one man's head alone, there it dwells as yet. One man alone of the whole world believes it; there is one man against all men. That *he* take a sword, and try to propagate with that, will do little for him. You must first get your sword!" But Carlyle might have been expected to consider that the real difficulty about Mohammed is not at all how he got twenty or a hundred or a thousand people to believe in him—any one almost can do that—but how he has come to establish a religion as widely extended and as permanent as our own. And I affirm that the man must shut his eyes to the broadest, most conspicuous facts of the history of Islam, who denies that the sword has been the great means of propagating this religion. St. Hilaire, with his usual penetration of judgment and precision of expression, puts the whole matter in a nutshell when he says, "Without Islam the Arabs had not been the conquerors of the world, but without war Islam itself had not been." I like the honesty as I admire the penetration of Abulwalid, who plainly declared, "My principles are faith in one God and in this"—laying his hand on his scimitar. Until Mohammed appealed to the sword his faith made very little way. His earliest disciples, Abu Bekr, Ali, Omar, were undoubtedly moved, partly by the influence of the truth, partly by the power Mohammed's personality had over them. But such men as these were not to be won every day, and had he been allowed to propagate his opinions freely there is no reasonable probability that he would have been influential beyond his own city and generation. It was his banishment from Mecca which made him the founder of a religion. It is with true instinct that Moslems accept the Hegira as their era. Accepted in Medina as a persecuted man, the inhabitants of that rival city found in his wrongs and in his claims no bad pretext for gratifying their jealousy and the Bedouin lust of plunder. In point of fact it is not the history of a religion, but the history of an adventurer, or at the best, of a civil revolution, one reads in scanning the life of Mohammed after the Hegira. There is nothing more remarkable about these early annals than the total absence of all religious inquiry and discussion. In the early annals of the Buddhist religion, we find its preachers endeavouring to awaken a mental and spiritual interest, and entering freely into prolonged discussions regarding life and the future. In the early annals of Christianity we read of mental perplexity and spiritual distress, often of years spent in inquiry and investigation, but in the Moslem annals all is different. Here converts are made on the field of battle with the sword at their throat. Tribes are in a single hour convinced of the truth of the new faith, because they have no alternative but extermination.[1]

In reading the rapid conquests of Syria, Egypt, Persia, and the brilliant and gallant deeds of the early Moslem warriors, one wholly forgets that there is any difficulty in accounting for the success of Islam. It is merely a repetition of what has occurred again and again in history when a new race appears on the field, and for a time carries everything before it, till it in turn is conquered by its own prosperity. The Arabs were seized with the passion which has at various times seized the Assyrians, the Persians, the Greeks, the Romans, the Goths, the French, almost every great race or nation, the passion of being master. Can any one suppose that it was the desire to see men enjoying the advantages of a true religion which animated

[1] The chapter in Hottinger's learned *Historia Orientalis*, entitled "De causis Muham. conservantibus," would have been much more profitable had it not been levelled at the Romanists.

Akbah, when, after crossing and conquering the entire north of Africa, he spurred his horse into the waves of the Atlantic and cried, "Great God! if my course were not stopped by this sea, I would still go on to the unknown kingdoms of the West, preaching the unity of Thy holy name, and putting to the sword the rebellious nations who worship any other gods than Thee."

Pity for the benighted condition of their fellows, that pity which lies at the root of all laudable propagation of one's faith, has scarcely at all, if at all, been exhibited by Moslems. Zeal for the glory of God did, I believe, in many instances, animate them, and the persuasion that all who fell in battle went straight to Paradise did much to make them unflinching and daring in battle. "Paradise is under the shadow of swords!" was their battle-cry. "I will come upon you," wrote their commander to the Persian king, "with men who love death as much as you love life." "Paradise is before you"—this was Khaled's pithy address to his troops before leading them to battle—"the devil and hell behind. Fight bravely, and you will secure the one; fly, and you will fall into the other." As Mr. Freeman remarks, "the ordinary and natural inducements of the soldier—average courage, average patriotism, average professional honour—could not possibly keep him up to a conflict with men whose whole spirit and motives savoured of the extraordinary and supernatural." Yet too much must not be made even of the fanaticism of the conquerors of Syria and Persia. This we believe would have availed them little had they not begun for the first time to feel their strength as a united people, and had they not been possessed by that *esprit de corps* which leads troops to victory, and had they not been naturally a fighting race. It was often the least fanatical among them who did the doughtiest deeds. Khaled, the sword of God, might conceal his thirst for battle under a thin veil of religion, but obviously he fought for fighting's sake: he was never happier than when dashing single-handed among a troop of infidels. It is no time to talk of religious enthusiasm or anything else but the love of the thing when you see Derar disobeying orders to engage thirty of the enemy single-handed, and leaving seventeen of them dead on the field. In an army which numbered many such men, and in which almost every man had been accustomed to plunder from his youth up, there was really not a great deal for fanaticism to do. From one city alone the caliph's fifth part of the spoil took 900 camels to transport it to Medina. Obviously there were other motives at work in such a war than the simple desire to propagate the faith.

At the same time, as the Romans were said to conquer like savages but to rule like philosophic statesmen, the advance of Islam was due not less to the admirably equitable and salutary government of the early caliphs than to the irresistible prowess of their troops. The impression which was made on the inhabitants and governors of conquered countries by the simple habits of these men, as well as by their integrity and devotion to the cause, went far to consolidate their empire. The establishment of the first caliph consisted of a single slave and one camel, and on accepting the caliphate, he ordered his daughter to take strict account of his patrimony that it might testify against him if he should be enriched by the office which he held for others' good, and not his own. His successor, Omar, made his triumphal entry into Jerusalem mounted on a red camel, with his whole camp furniture slung across his saddle-bow in the shape of a sack, one end of which held his dates, and the other his rice. Before him hung a leathern water-bottle, and behind him a wooden platter; and beyond this simple equipment he needed nothing. "Why," asked the Emperor Heraclius, "does he go in patched clothes, and not richly clad like other princes?"

"Because," replied some of the faithful, "he cares only for the world to come, and seeks favour in the eyes of God alone." "In what kind of a palace does he reside?" asked the emperor. "In a house built of mud." "Who are his attendants?" "Beggars and the poor." "What tapestry does he sit upon?"—but here evidently the story becomes legendary.—"Justice and equity." "What is his throne?" "Abstinence and true knowledge." "What is his treasure?" "Trust in God." "And what his guard?" "The bravest of the unitarians."

To nations which had groaned under heavy taxation, and yet received in return no single advantage of good government, it seemed pleasant and hopeful to submit to men who themselves were but servants of a great cause. The Romans had attached to themselves all their useful and faithful allies by rewarding their services with Roman citizenship; the Moslems did not even require that men should show themselves worthy of being enrolled in the number of the faithful, but offered to all conditions of men equality with themselves on the spot. They only required a prompt, immediate decision. The Koran, Tribute, or the Sword, these were the alternatives offered to all the world. If any preferred to retain their own religion, they might do so by paying tribute; if they declined to be either Moslems or tributaries of Moslems, the sword alone could settle it. And the very promptitude with which this alternative was pressed contributed greatly to the success of Islam. A grey-headed Christian priest listening to a sermon of Omar's hinted that he was in error. "Strike off that old man's head," said the caliph quietly, "if he repeats his words." Such was the summary, unflinching rule that was felt through the whole empire. When Ziyad entered on the government of Bassora he found the place a mere den of robbers and assassins. He gave notice that he meant to rule with the sword, and that all persons found strolling in the city after evening prayers should be put to death. Two hundred persons forfeited their lives the first night, five the second, and subsequently the city was a model of security and peace. Under this strong-handed government other conquered districts, which had been notorious for lawlessness, became so safe and well conducted that the people did not even close their doors at night, but merely set a hurdle across the doorway to keep out the cattle.

Again, the extreme simplicity of the creed of Islam greatly favoured its rapid propagation. No elaborate explanations were required to teach the ignorant: the rude negro could understand it on its first recital, and it could be administered at the point of the sword amidst the press of battle. It demanded no long noviciate; the unhorsed Persian who had fallen to the ground a fire-worshipper might rise from under the lance-point of the Arab a fully privileged Moslem. It was a creed for which the human mind has an instinctive affinity, and which has never roused abhorrence even in the mind of a polytheist. To men who had begun to despair of finding truth amidst the bewildering subtleties of a metaphysical theology, it was a relief to find themselves face to face with a simple creed, and to be compelled to believe it.

> "In the fresh passions of a vigorous race
> Was sown a living seed;
> Strong these contending mysteries to displace
> By one plain ancient creed."

All these features of the propagation of Islam make its success thoroughly intelligible. Its creed was simple, easily understood, unencumbered by observances, and not glaringly false. It was offered by men who held their own lives cheap, and other men's still cheaper, and who, with the Koran in one hand and the scimitar in the other, demanded an immediate decision. Its terms were generous, granting at once to those who accepted it every privilege of the Moslem scarred and grey in the service of the

Prophet. It offered a connection with the most promising cause then in the world; and not only at once conferred freedom, equality, and all the benefits of a strong-handed government, but opened paths to position, wealth, and honours.

Having thus won its way to empire by means not altogether though partly commendable, the influence of Mohammedanism on the world at large has been neither wholly good nor wholly evil. In some respects it has retarded, while in others it has signally advanced what is conveniently, if somewhat vaguely, termed civilization. There is nothing in the religion itself which is antagonistic to mental culture, although the instinct of self-preservation has produced a sensitive jealousy of anything like free thought in connection with its theology.

It has been the boast of Islam that it embraces sects representing every shade of opinion, and undoubtedly its creed gains both emphasis and comprehensiveness from its brevity. These sects, it is true, have more than once endeavoured to exterminate one another with the sword, and theologians who have shown the speculative tendencies of an Abelard or an Erigena, have been as liable to persecution in Islam as those philosophers were in Christendom. Averroes himself, by far the greatest of

Arabic philosophers, was compelled to do penance for his errors by sitting in the mosque, while the worshippers were expected to testify to their own orthodoxy by spitting in his face,—a form of religious persecution which, as recent events have proved, is not yet obsolete in Islam. Commanders of the faithful, supreme in all besides, have been reminded that in this direction they were fettered. Mamoun, one of the most munificent patrons of learning,[1] was suspected of *Zendikism*; while Vathek spent a troubled reign because he denied the eternity of the Koran. At the same time, this narrowness and bigotry cannot be laid to the charge of the creed itself. The creed which is satisfied by a man's adherence to the one article of "God revealed by His prophets," if it does not bring the impulse and the light which might result from greater accuracy and detail, at least leaves the amplest scope for speculation. And the religion which assigned the martyr's crown to every soldier who fell in battle for the cause, and yet proclaimed that the "ink of the scholar was more precious than the blood of the martyr," can scarcely with justice be branded as obscurantist.[2]

[1] Hottinger's *Hist. Orientalis*, p. 580.

[2] The instructive pages of Gobineau on this subject will well repay perusal. *Les Religions*, &c., pp. 24–28.

It was only to be expected that the severe monotheism of the Saracens would brook no contamination with the profuse polytheism and licentious mythology of Greece and Rome. No accuracy of thought, no delicate finish of language, could compensate for the stain of error that blots the page of the classical writers. The colourless writings of Hippocrates, Galen, Euclid, and Aristotle, were freely translated and widely read; but even the liberal son of the splendid Harun Al Rashid, when he preferred to bring books instead of captives as his spoils from conquered Greece, left behind him in contempt the plays of Sophocles and Æschylus, the orations of Demosthenes, the histories of Thucydides and Herodotus—all in fact which would have opened a new world to the Eastern mind. If this was so in the golden age of Saracen history, we can scarcely discredit the story of Amru burning the Alexandrian library by order of the caliph. "If the books of the Greeks," said Omar, "agree with the Koran, they are superfluous; if they disagree, they are dangerous, and must be destroyed"—a saying which, if not uttered by Omar, is at least full of historical verisimilitude and significance.[1]

But, in the main, education up to a certain

[1] Gibbon discredits the story; Von Hammer receives it.

point—literature in certain departments, and science in some of its branches—have been materially promoted by the mental awakening produced by Islam. The Arabian mind had always shown itself lively and intelligent, and susceptible of culture, especially in an emotional and imaginative direction.[1] The Koran gave an extraordinary impulse to this pre-existing capability. It was better than an enactment of compulsory education, for it became the book of the people, and to be able to read was now an object of pious ambition. To recite the Koran was a work of merit. Alongside of the mosques, schools or colleges were built, or the work of instruction was carried on inside the sacred building itself. "To learn to read," they said, "is worth more than fasting; to teach it, is more meritorious than prayer."[2] Mohammed himself used to

[1] Dozy declares that the Arabs are "le peuple le moins inventif du monde" (*Histoire*, i. 12). Though idolaters, they had no mythology; and after they gave themselves to scientific pursuits, "ils ont montré la même absence de puissance créatrice. Ils ont traduit et commenté les ouvrages des anciens ; ils ont enrichi certaines spécialités par des observations patientes, exactes, minutieuses ; mais ils n'ont rien inventé, on ne leur doit aucune idée grande et féconde."

[2] Oelsner, *Des Effets*, &c., p. 208, from whose admirable account of the learning of the Saracens many of the facts here stated are derived.

say, "Teach your children poetry; it opens the mind, lends grace to wisdom, and makes the heroic virtues hereditary." And, what was more to the purpose, when living in Medina among a poorly educated population, he gave liberty to every Meccan prisoner who taught twelve boys of Medina the art of writing.[1] And within a comparatively short time after Mohammed, there were crowded universities at Baghdad, Damascus, Alexandria, Bassora, and Samarkand; and probably at no period of the world's history was literature so richly rewarded as under some of the Abbasside princes. The victor at the poetic contests received 100 pieces of gold, a horse, an embroidered caftan, and a lovely slave; and, apparently in one gift, Abu Taman received from his sovereign 50,000 pieces of gold. But it was not in pure literature that the work of the Saracens was of greatest service to the world, but rather in the departments of medicine, philosophy, and the mathematical sciences. In medicine their work has never been adequately appraised, because barely three European students have carefully studied their medical books. But their influence on the study of chemistry, algebra, and astronomy, is visible in the very terminology of these sciences.

[1] Sprenger, iii. 131.

The arts of statuary and painting were denounced by the early Moslems as incentives to idolatry, and even yet a few of their doctors forbid the delineation of anything that has life, under pain of being cast into hell. But this iconoclastic austerity long ago gave way; and while the statues of men are still forbidden, other works of art are allowed, except in the mosques.[1] Music, though condemned by the Prophet, had too rooted a place in human nature to be abandoned; and if we are to credit all accounts of their influence, the Saracen musicians must have brought their art to a high state of efficiency.[2]

In philosophy the attainments of the Arabians have probably been overrated rather than depreciated.[3] As middle-men, or transmitters, indeed, their importance can scarcely be too

[1] Burton's *Pilgr.* i. 137; Syed Ali's *Crit. Exam.* 331; Lane's *Mod. Egyp.* ii. 2.

[2] Berington's *Lit. Hist. of Middle Ages*, 426.

[3] This is the opinion of Berington (*Lit. Hist. of Middle Ages*, p. 455), who sums up a pretty full and interesting account of Saracenic learning with the remark that it "has experienced too much prodigality of praise;" and even Oelsner admits that the results are somewhat disappointing. Freeman, too, thinks he discerns a prevalent disposition to assert for the Saracens an untrue monopoly of excellence in science and philosophy, and calls attention to the fact that many of the most famous literary men at the court of the caliphs were not Mohammedans at all, but Jews or Christians.

highly estimated. They were keen students of Aristotle when the very language in which he wrote was unknown in Roman Christendom; and the commentaries of Averroes on the most exact of Greek philosophers are said to be worthy of the text. It was at the Mohammedan university in his native city of Cordova, and from Arabian teachers, that this precursor of Spinoza derived those germs of thought whose fruit may be seen in the whole history of scholastic theology. And just before Averroes entered these learned halls, a young man passed from them, equipped with the same learning, and gifted with a genius and penetration of judgment which have made his opinions final wherever the name of Maimonides is known. Undoubtedly these two fellow-citizens—the Arabic-speaking Mohammedan and the Arabic-speaking Jew—have left their mark deep on all subsequent Jewish and Christian learning. And even though it be doubted whether their influence has been wholly beneficial, they may well be claimed as instances of the intellectual ardour which Mohammedan learning could inspire or awaken.

A recent writer of great promise in the philosophy of religion has assigned to the Arab thinkers the honourable function of creating modern philosophy. "Theology and philosophy became in the hands of the Moors fused and blended; the Greek scientific theory as to the origin of things interwound with the Hebrew faith in a Creator. And so speculation became in a new and higher sense theistic; and the interpretation of the universe the explication of God's relation to it and its relation to God."[1] But speculation had become theistic long before there was an Arab philosophy. The same questions which form the staple of modern philosophy were discussed at Alexandria three centuries before Mohammed; and there is scarcely a Christian thinker of the third or fourth century who does not write in presence of the great problem of God's connection with the world, the relation of the Infinite to the finite, of the unseen intangible Spirit to the crass material universe. What we have here to do with, however, is not to ascertain whether modern philosophy be truly the offspring of the unexpected marriage of Aristotle and the Koran, but whether the religion promulgated in the latter is or is not obstructive of intellectual effort and enlightenment. And enough has been said to show that there is nothing in the religion which necessarily and directly tends to obstruct either philosophy or science, though when we consider the history and achievements

[1] Fairbairn's *Studies*, p. 398.

of that race which has for six centuries been the leading representative of Islam, we are inclined to add that there is nothing in the religion which necessarily leads on the mind to the highest intellectual efforts. Voltaire, in his own nervous way, exclaims, "I detest the Turks, as the tyrants of their wives and the enemies of the arts." And the religion has shown an affinity for such uncivilized races. It has not taken captive any race which possesses a rich literature, nor has it given birth to any work of which the world demands a translation; and precisely in so far as individuals have shown themselves possessed of great speculative and creative genius, have they departed from the rigid orthodoxy of the Koran. We should conclude therefore that the outburst of literary and scientific enthusiasm in the eighth century was due, not directly to the influence of the Mohammedan religion, but to the mental awakening and exultant consciousness of power and widened horizon that came to the conquering Saracens. At first their newly-awakened energy found scope in other fields than that of philosophy. "Marte undique obstrepente, musis vix erat locus."[1] But when the din of war died down, the voice of the Muses was heard,

[1] Dr. Hunt's Oration *De Antiq. Ling. Arab.* quoted by Inchbald, p. 37

and the same fervour which had made the Saracen arms irresistible was spent now in the acquirement of knowledge.[1]

Tolerance has frequently been claimed as one of the virtues of Islam, but, we think, erroneously. A religion which punishes apostasy with death can scarcely claim to be a tolerant religion. It is true that there have been some most notable exemplifications of tolerance among Mohammedans. When the pertinacious and over-zealous Raymond Lully had worn out the patience of his Mohammedan hosts by his arguments in favour of Christianity, and when they had resolved to silence him by death, he was defended by one of the Saracen muftis. This admirable specimen of the tolerance of theology remarked "that as they would praise the zeal of a Mohammedan who should go among the Christians for the purpose of converting them to the true faith, so they could not but honour in a Christian the same zeal for the spread of that religion which appeared to him to be the true one."[2] But the whole

[1] Rénan, one of the few authorities qualified by first-hand acquaintance with the subject to pronounce a judgment, considers Islamism incompatible with the highest development of science and philosophy. "Incapable de se transformer et d'admettre aucun élément de vie civile et profane, l'islamisme arracha de son sein tout germe de culture rationelle." See *Averroes*, p. iii.

[2] Neander, *Hist. of Church*, vii. 90. For other instances, Freeman's *Lectures*, 2nd ed. p. 153.

spirit of the religion is counter to these individual instances. Our most reliable authorities, such observers as Lane and Burton, assure us that the toleration which many Moslems show is mere superficial politeness. The children are taught formulas in which they may compendiously curse Jews, Christians, and all unbelievers. At the same time they exercise remarkable self-control, and do not forget what is due to their own dignity; and, as Lady Duff Gordon's experience proves, they will show themselves more tolerant to those who treat them tolerantly.[1]

And if not remarkable for charity to unbelievers, they are singularly long-suffering towards one another. One who spent many years among them writes: "I have often heard an Egyptian say, on receiving a blow from an equal, 'God bless thee!' 'God requite thee good!' 'Beat me again!' In general a quarrel terminates by one or both parties saying, 'Justice is against me!' Often, after this, they recite

[1] The true account of this feature of Islam is given with his usual knowledge and impartiality by Dozy, who says (*Histoire*, ii. 50), "Il arriva en Espagne ce qui arriva dans tous les pays que les Arabes avaient conquis : leur domination, de douce et d'humaine qu'elle avait été au commencement, dégénéra en un despotisme intolérable." Instances of very gross intolerance on the part of Moslem governments are given in the same volume, pp. 108, 9.

the Fathah together, and then sometimes embrace and kiss one another."[1] And just as we speak of Christian charity and Christian meekness, so, when they wish to say that any one is humble, meek, and charitable, they say he has "Moslem feelings;" "The meekness of a Moslem."[2] And this meekness is all the more striking because it exists alongside of the manly independence and fortitude which undoubtedly the religion tends to produce.

But as we endeavour to estimate the good and evil of Islam, it gradually appears that the chief point we must attend to is to distinguish between its value to Arabia in the seventh century and its value to the world at large. No one, I presume, would deny that to Mohammed's contemporaries his religion was an immense advance on anything they had previously believed in. It welded together the disunited tribes, and lifted the nation to the forefront of the important powers in the world. It effected what Christianity and Judaism had alike failed to effect—it swept away, once and for ever, idolatry, and established the idea of one supreme God. Its influence on Arabia was justly and pathetically put by the Moslem refugees in Abyssinia, who, when required to say why they

[1] Lane, i. 386.

[2] Lady Duff Gordon's *Letters*, p. 257.

should not be sent back to Mecca, gave the following account of their religion and what it had done for them. "O king, we were plunged in ignorance and barbarism; we worshipped idols; we ate dead bodies; we committed lewdness; disregarded family ties and the duties of neighbourhood and hospitality; we knew no law but that of the strong, when God sent among us a messenger of whose birth, truthfulness, integrity, and innocence, we were aware; and he called us to the unity of God, and taught us not to associate any god with Him; he forbade us the worship of idols, and enjoined upon us to speak the truth, to be faithful to our trusts, to be merciful, and to regard the rights of others; to love our relatives and to protect the weak; to flee vice and avoid all evil. He taught us to offer prayers, to give alms, and to fast. And because we believed in him and obeyed him, therefore are we persecuted and driven from our country to seek thy protection."

The radical vice of Mohammedanism lies far deeper than any mere blot on its morality or error in its doctrinal teaching. It is an anachronism. It is an ignorant attempt to insert into a series of acknowledged revelations an assumed revelation which is incongruous and out of date. Islam claims to be a historical religion, a religion which has regard to God's historical connection with the world, and yet it has thoroughly misapprehended its own place in history. It owes its success, in large measure, to its appropriation of preceding revelations, but, through ignorance of the real history and relation of these revelations, it has so bungled this appropriation, as to stultify itself and work mischief on earth.

Its defenders are fond of comparing it with Judaism, in order to bring out that its morality is at least as high, and its legislation at least as advanced and just, as that of Moses. But this line of defence betrays ignorance of the grand distinction between the two religions. Mohammedanism claims to be final and complete; Mosaism distinctly disclaimed both finality and completeness. "A prophet," said Moses, "shall the Lord your God raise up unto you, like unto me." Every part of the Mosaic religion had a forward look, and was designed to leave the mind in an attitude of suspense and expectation. Accommodations were made to the weakness and immaturity of the people, which were abolished in their adult strength. Mosaism must therefore be judged according to its own claims as a temporary and local religion, as the mere pædagogue slave leading men to the teacher but not itself uttering the final truth. But Islam, claiming to be final and universal, must be judged as such; and professing as it does to supersede not only Judaism but also Christianity, it must be condemned by every point in which we find it a retrogression and not an advance on our own religion. The accommodations to a rude and untaught tribe which are judicious, seasonable, and helpful, as a temporary expedient, are an insufferable offence to morality when proclaimed as the ultimate law of conscience. The institutions, such as pilgrimage, which are at least harmless, and probably conducive to unity in a local religion, become a ridiculous burden when proclaimed as binding on the whole race. The reforms of Mohammed, such as the restriction of polygamy, were good and useful for his own time and place, but by making them final, he has prevented further progress, consecrated immorality, and permanently established half-measures. What were restrictions to his Arabs would have been license to other men.[1] "Considered as delivered only to pagan Arabs, the religious,

[1] "When Islam penetrates to countries lower in the scale of humanity than were the Arabs of Mohammed's day, it suffices to elevate them to that level. But it does so at a tremendous cost. It reproduces in its new converts the characteristics of its first—their impenetrable self-esteem, their unintelligent scorn, and blind hatred of all other creeds. And thus the capacity for all other advance is destroyed."—Osborn's *Islam under the Arabs*, p. 93.

moral, and civil precepts of the Koran are admirable. The error of their author was in delivering them to others besides pagan Arabs," and in giving to temporary expedients a sanction which has erected them into permanent laws. A writer who has studied the matter with the insight of a widely-informed historian, says: "The temporary and partial reform effected by Islam has proved the surest obstacle to fuller and more permanent reform. A Mahometan nation accepts a certain amount of truth, receives a certain amount of civilization, practises a certain amount of toleration. But all these are so many obstacles to the acceptance of truth, civilization, and toleration in their perfect shape."[1]

In plain terms, Mohammed was an ignorant man—a man so ignorant that he did not know his own ignorance. Knowing nothing of the government, policy, or law of Rome, to which all the civilized world has paid its tribute of respect, he presumed that the code of Justinian ought to be superseded by the fragmentary ideas he had jotted down on palm-leaves and mutton bones and thrown higgledy-piggledy into a chest. Knowing nothing of Christianity, and never having even read the canonical Gospels, he imagined he had more to say for the world's

[1] Freeman's *Lectures*, p. 51.

good than had fallen from the lips and shone from the life of Jesus Christ. Had his religion preceded Christianity, or had he never enjoyed the means of informing himself regarding it, some apology might have been devised for his extreme presumption in aspiring to the sovereignty of the world in things civil and spiritual. Nay, we will go further, and say that had Mohammed preceded Christianity, or had he not proclaimed his own religion as final, it might have been a blessing of the most extensive kind to the world. Doctrinally and morally it is a half-way house between heathenism and Christianity, but practically it can never serve as such, because it claims to be itself an advance upon Christianity, and final. It is this claim that has choked it throughout. The dead hand of the short-sighted author of the Koran is on the throat of every Mohammedan nation. And it is this claim which stultifies it in the view of any one who has studied other religions. It bears the marks of immaturity on every part of it. It proves itself to be a religion only for the childhood of a race, by its minute prescriptions, its detailed precepts, its observances, its appeals to fear. It does not even recognise that there is a higher religion, that the only true religion is a religion of liberty and of the spirit.

Here is the judgment of one who has spent a large part of his life among Mohammedans, and seven years of it in a careful study of their history.

"There are to be found," he says, "in Mohammedan history all the elements of greatness—faith, courage, endurance, self-sacrifice. But enclosed within the narrow walls of a rude theology, and a barbarous polity, from which the capacity to grow and the liberty to modify have been sternly cut off, they work no deliverance upon the earth. They are strong only for destruction. When that work is over, they either prey upon each other, or beat themselves to death against the bars of their own prison-house. No permanent dwelling-place can be erected on a foundation of sand; and no durable or humanising polity upon a foundation of fatalism, despotism, polygamy, and slavery. When Muhammadan states cease to be racked by revolutions, they succumb to the poison diffused by a corrupt moral atmosphere. A Durwesh, ejaculating 'Allah!' and revolving in a series of rapid gyrations until he drops senseless, is an exact image of the course of their history."[1]

Or, hear the conclusion of a very different writer, who has given the most favourable view of Islam that can reasonably be given.

[1] Osborn's *Islam under the Arabs*, pp. 94, 95

"Thus in the faiths old heathendom that shook
Were different powers of strife;
Mohammed's truth lay in a holy Book,
Christ's in a sacred Life.

So while the world rolls on from change to change,
And realms of thought expand,
The Letter stands without expanse or range,
Stiff as a dead man's hand;

While as the life-blood fills the growing form,
The Spirit Christ has shed
Flows through the ripening ages fresh and warm,
More felt than heard or read.

And, therefore, though ancestral sympathies,
And closest ties of race,
May guard Mohammed's precepts and decrees
Through many a tract of space;

Yet in the end the tight-drawn line must break,
The sapless tree must fall,
Nor let the form one time did well to take
Be tyrant over all."

III.

BUDDHISM.

"*Sauf le Christ tout seul, il n'est point, parmi les fondateurs de religion, de figure plus pure ni plus touchante que celle du Bouddha.*"
SAINT HILAIRE.

III.

I CHOOSE Buddhism as a representative religion, because, if you will allow the paradox, it can only by courtesy be termed a religion at all.[1] It does not, like other religions, start from some conception of a supernatural world to which man must somehow adjust himself; it does not aim, like other religions, at bringing man into harmony with God; but it sets itself manfully to solve the problem of human existence and to find deliverance from moral and physical evil, and in doing so it does not find itself compelled to recognise God at any point of the process. In its attitude towards the idea of a Personal God it resembles modern Agnosticism, but its whole motive was earnestly ethical. The popular religion of India, which Buddhism for a while competed with and almost superseded, had

[1] "In real fact, Buddhism ought not to be called a religion at all, for where there is no god, there can be no need," &c.—Monier Williams, *Indian Wisdom*, p. 57.

entirely disassociated the ideas of religion and morality. The priests had never been the social moralists to whom men looked for instruction in matters of conduct, neither had they in their own lives shown that there is any necessary connection between the service of God and personal purity. A similar state of matters in the history of the religion of Rome at last produced a reaction against the priesthood, and gave rise to a very elevated school of moralists, of which Plutarch and Dion, Epictetus and Marcus Aurelius, are the well-known representatives. So in India there came a time when the people were prepared to admit the insufficiency of ceremonial to purge them from sin, and responded to a teaching which, though it told them nothing of God, was yet in all other respects true to the deepest convictions of their own moral nature. Sakya-muni did not set himself in declared opposition to the whole popular faith; he was neither a scoffer, nor, on all points, a dogmatic controversialist. Like his Roman fellow-labourers, he was not so concerned to explode the popular opinions about gods supreme and subordinate, as to show them the way to emancipation from evil by righteousness and charity. The words of Seneca might with slight alteration have fallen from his lips: "Would you know what it is that philosophy promises? I answer, Practical advice. The lost, the dying, stretch their hands towards you, they implore you, they cast upon you all their hopes. They entreat you to draw them forth from such abject misery, to show them their errors, and enlighten their perplexities by the bright shining of the truth. Tell them, then, what nature declares to be necessary, and what superfluous; how easy her laws; how pleasant life and how free to those who accept them; how bitter and perplexed to those who follow their own fancies rather." It was in this character that Sakya-muni presented himself to men. He described himself as "the father and mother of his helpless children, their guide and leader along the precipitous path of life; shedding the light of his truth like the sun and moon in the vault of heaven; providing a ferry-boat for passengers over this vain sea of shadows; as a propitious rain-cloud, restoring all things to life; providing salvation and refuge, by directing men into the final path that leads to the eternal city."[1] But not only did Buddha leave room for a religion, and secure that religion should above all else be moral and practical, but in point of fact it is as a religion and not as a philosophy

[1] Beal's *Buddhist Scriptures*, p. 137

that Buddhism has been received and is now adhered to by a full third of the human race.

Buddhism arose in India in the sixth century B.C., but in the religious stratification of that eminently religious and productive country it is by no means the earliest layer. Three religions preceded it: the wild devil-worship of the aborigines, which still, with its significant redeeming features, lingers among the Sudras and hill-tribes; the religion of the Aryan invaders, which is represented in the Vedic hymns, and which has been described as "a naturalism with a nascent sacerdotalism superinduced;"[1] and finally Brahmanism, which was this nascent sacerdotalism fully developed, especially in its distinctive features of priestly mediation, caste, and pantheism.

Whether the pantheism of the Brahmanical religion arose from the priestly craving to identify their own caste more closely with the Deity than others, or whether it was evolved by the theosophic speculators who started, in accordance with their race instincts, from an abstract conception which excluded, alike as regards God and man, the notion of personality, it is difficult to say.[2] Probably both influences

[1] Fairbairn's *Studies*, p. 130.

[2] Fairbairn's *Studies* give an admirably lucid and profound sketch of the growth of Brahmanism. Cf. Pfleiderer's *Religion*, ii.

were at work. What concerns us is to note that the doctrines of emanation and transmigration were both the necessary outcome of this pantheistic conception. All things have emanated from Brahma; all must return to him again. "As the threads from the spider, the tree from the seed, the fire from the coal, the stream from the fountain, *the waves from the sea*, so is the world produced out of Brahma." "It is with us when we enter the Divine Spirit as if a lump of salt was thrown into the sea: it becomes dissolved into the water from which it was produced, and is not to be taken out again." But this absorption is regulated. Those who have served and *known* Brahma will be absorbed into him at death; those who have not done so must pass through a purgatory proportioned to their guilt. They seized upon the great principle that the punishment is of the same nature as the guilt, the reward as the merit; or, in their own expressive and far-reaching maxim, "A man is born into the world he has made." To the guilt contracted in former lives he must trace all the sorrows that afflict him here. The *lex talionis* is carried out with the most horrifying exactness, and with a wealth of realistic invention which Dante might have envied. He who has killed a Brahman, after paying the first instalments of his penalty by suffering protracted tortures in a graduated series of hells, will be born again in this world as a boar, an ass, a goat, or an outcast, according to the degree of his guilt. He who has stolen gold from a Brahman will be born again with diseased nails. If he has been a drunkard, he will be born with discoloured teeth. If it is grain that has tempted a man's thievish propensities, he shall be reborn as a rat; if he has shown a partiality for fruit, he shall live again as an ape. And thus only by passing through an almost endless succession of punishments and births and revolting experiences could man win his slow way back to a welcome extinction in Brahma. Nothing could tell more powerfully on the popular imagination than the future thus depicted—a future, the reality of which seemed to be vouched for by the very facts of the present life.

The good side of this view of the future there is no space here to enlarge upon. It was unfortunately the evil tendencies of it which were chiefly developed. Two things resulted from it. The Brahmans, without whom no sacrifice could be performed, and no deliverance from the alarming prospect effected, gained absolute supremacy, and religion in consequence became more and more a matter of ceremony, less and less a matter of morality. Secondly, as in a pantheistic system there can be no absolute immortality of individuals, and as all persons must eventually be absorbed in the impersonal existence, the rewards and punishments of men must have a limit. Reward as well as punishment must terminate. But so long as men do good they deserve reward, as they deserve punishment so long as they do evil. Works of all kinds, therefore, must be got rid of. Man's highest state is the state of contemplative abstraction, in which nothing is done. Here is the doctrine as it appears in various passages of the Upanishads. "As flowing rivers are resolved into the sea, losing their names and forms, so the *wise*, freed from name and form, pass into the Divine Spirit, which is greater than the great. He who *knows* that supreme Spirit, becomes spirit." "Whoever knows this, 'I am Brahma,' knows all. Even the gods are unable to prevent his becoming Brahma." "Know him, the Spirit, to be one alone. Give up all words contrary to this. He is the bridge of immortality." "Crossing this bridge, the blind cease to be blind, the wounded to be wounded, the afflicted to be afflicted; and on crossing this bridge nights become days, for ever-refulgent is the region of the universal Spirit." Salvation, that is to say, is to be obtained by priestly rites and transcendental knowledge.

Now, whatever profound thoughts lay about the roots of Brahmanism, and however suitable to the Hindu mind it may originally have been, there can be no question that it held the people of India, as it still holds them, in a bondage at once tyrannical and degrading. It was against the demoralising ceremonialism and the despotic exclusiveness of this sacerdotal religion that the revolt at last came in the form of Buddhism. Analogous to Christianity in many respects, Buddhism resembles it in its historical origin. Both religions had their roots in an exclusive sacerdotal religion, and both proclaimed deliverance to all without distinction of caste or race. The sufferings of men which the Brahmans had used to confirm their own supremacy and illustrate the permanence of caste distinctions, roused in the sympathetic heart of Buddha a feeling of kindred with all men, and a purpose to deliver himself and them at any cost. And as the method of deliverance was elaborated by his own experience and thought, it is best understood when we learn the outline of his life and the ideas which formed it. And although the material out of which such an outline can now be sketched is almost entirely legendary, yet legendary as it is, I believe it will leave on the mind substantially the right impression of this certainly historical person.[1]

The names by which he is most commonly designated, Sakya-muni and Buddha,[2] are titles which he acquired; the former meaning the Sage[3] of the Sakya tribe, and the Buddha meaning the Enlightened. His own name was Siddartha, and his family name Gautama. He was the son of Suddhodana, a rajah of the Sakya tribe, who reigned in Kapilavastu, a few days' journey north of Benares. There is some rea-

[1] "It seems not impossible, after all, that Sakya-muni is an unreal being, and that all that is related of him is as much a fiction as is that of his preceding migrations, and the miracles that attended his birth, his life, and his departure."—Wilson's *Works*, ii. 346. M. Senart (*Essai sur la légende du Buddha*, Paris, 1875) claims to have sifted the legends thoroughly, and his answer to the question, How much of a historical character remains? is "Bien peu assurément" (p. 509).

[2] Those who have any curiosity to see the other numerous names and titles of the Buddha may consult Wilson's *Works*, ii. 9, 10, and Hardy's *Manual of Buddhism*, p. 354.

[3] The Dhammapada (268, 269) says: "A man is not a Muni because he observes silence, if he is foolish and ignorant; but the wise who, taking the balance, chooses the good and avoids evil, he is a Muni, and is a Muni thereby; he who in this world weighs both sides is called a Muni." To which Max Müller appends the statement that Muni means a Sage, and comes from "man," to think; and from "muni" comes "manna," silence.—Buddhaghosha's *Parables*, p. 133.

son to believe that these Sakyas were not of Aryan, but of Turanian descent,[1] and this, were it established, would account for his ability to emancipate himself from the idea of caste under which the Hindu mind lay helpless. And unquestionably it is among the Turanians that Buddhism has found most acceptance: although, in presence of the fact that Christianity, of Semitic origin, has been most cordially received by people of Aryan race, this may not be considered evidence of much weight. It is of more importance to observe that Buddhism at a very early period in its history showed a tendency to ally itself with the devil-worship which characterized many of the existing Turanian religions.

The voluntary incarnation of Buddha is a myth of later formation, and one of many in which there exists a very striking, and, it must be owned, perplexing similarity to the most striking points in our Lord's career.[2] It would seem that he grew up to all outward appearance very like other young rajahs, dividing his time between the relaxing luxuries of an oriental palace and the invigorating exercises and athletic

[1] Beal's *Buddhist Scriptures*, p. 127. Wilson's *Works*, ii. 345. But comp. Hodgson's *Essays*, p. 123.

[2] The references to Buddhism by the early Christian fathers, and some hints on the connection between the two religions, will be found in Wilson's *Works*, ii. 312.

contests in which he outdid all competition. But he was born with an eye for suffering and a heart for suffering, and through all the glitter of his luxurious and magnificent life his keen sight penetrated to the coarse and wasting fabric which it overlaid; through the soft strains of musicians and Natch-girls he heard the moans of those who lay in the outer darkness; through the perfumes of his gardens and halls the smell of death struck on his sense; between his brooding spirit and all the pride of life with which he was studiously surrounded there floated without ceasing visions of decay and dissolution, of ghastly suffering and never-ending bondage. The growth of this distaste for pleasures that could not last, of this yearning for an eternal rest, is depicted in a striking and well-known legend. One day when the prince was going out by the eastern gate of the city to his pleasure-garden he met on the way a decrepit old man, leaning heavily on a stick and trembling in every limb, his veins standing out on his emaciated body, his teeth gone or loose, and his voice broken and quavering. "What is this?" said the prince anxiously to the charioteer. "Is this condition peculiar to this man or to his family?" "By no means, my lord," replied the driver. "This is old age; suffering and toil have broken this man's strength, and he is now scorned by his kindred, and left without support, like a dead tree in the forest. And this comes to all men; your father, your mother, every creature must come to this." "Alas!" said the prince, "how ignorant and mistaken is man, who is proud of the youth which intoxicates him, and sees not the old age which awaits him. Turn back to the city, what have I to do with pleasure, who am destined to such an end?"

Another time, going out by the south gate to his pleasure-garden, he saw on the road a man seized with sickness, lying without shelter and without companion, gasping and cramped, and with dismay in his face. Having again heard from his charioteer that this was no peculiar condition, but a calamity to which all men are liable, he once more felt the incongruity of pleasure-seeking, and returned to the city. Similarly, a third time, he met on the road a funeral procession, the dead man stretched stark on his bier, and the relatives throwing dust on their heads, beating their breasts, and uttering piercing lamentations. "Alas for youth," said the prince, "which old age destroys! Alas for health which sickness invades! Alas for life which ends in death! Oh, that there were no old age; no sickness; no death. Let us go back. I will meditate how to accomplish deliverance."

This determination was confirmed by a fourth spectacle. This was a bhikshu, or mendicant, walking with the placid expression of a disciplined spirit, wearing his single poor garment with dignity, and carrying in his hand his alms-bowl. The prince's interpreter, the driver, explained to him that this man walks through life with calmness because he has renounced its pleasures, and has forced himself to conquer himself, and lives now without passion, without envy, without desire. "This," said the prince, "is the way of escape. I also will renounce life and its pleasures."

This resolution was vehemently opposed by his father and the courtiers. But the very means they took to entangle him more deeply in pleasures contributed to his emancipation. For, awaking one night, and rising from the couch where he had gone to sleep in contempt of the Natch-dancers, he saw the lamps untrimmed, smoky, and defiled with oil; and the sleeping women themselves lying about in unseemly positions, some grinding their teeth, others dribbling from their mouth, or uneasily moving and muttering.[1] This was final. "Never again," he vowed, "will I indulge in the pleasures of sense; never again—this is the

[1] Bigandet, *Life of Gaudama*, p. 55. Beal's *Romantic Hist. of Buddha*, p. 130.

last time; from henceforth I entertain such thoughts no more." Going to his wife's chamber, he gazed a farewell to her and his infant heir, then summoned his groom, mounted his horse, and forsook once for all his home, his kindred, his kingdom, and every worldly possession. Riding all night, he halted only when pursuit was impossible, and halted then only to make his "great renunciation" complete by giving his royal mantle and circlet of pearls to his faithful and remonstrating servant, and by cutting off with his sword the long locks of the warrior, thus reducing himself wholly to the condition of mere undistinguished humanity.

But though thus strong in his resolve, Siddartha was only tasting the hardships and difficulties that beset his path from this his twenty-ninth year, till in his thirty-sixth year he won the peace he sought. The great tempter Mara, though roughly repulsed for the time, congratulates himself with the thought, "Sooner or later some lustful or malicious or angry thought must arise in his mind: in that moment I shall be his master." And "as a shadow follows the body, so from that day," says the chronicle, "did Mara follow the blessed one, striving to throw every obstacle in his way towards the Buddhahood." Not only did his royal palate nauseate the food that was first offered to him as a mendicant, but the ties of home, though so sternly cut, left wounds not soon healed. His father offered him the kingdom if he would return. "Dear son," he said, "the practice of religion involves as a first principle a loving, compassionate heart for all creatures; and for this reason the very name of a religious life is given to it. Why, then, should you consider a religious life as a term applied only to those who dwell in the lonely mountains? In former days men lived at home and practised religion. They did not then cast away their jewels, or shave their crowns, and yet they were able to attain to complete emancipation." But to all such remonstrances his son had but one answer: "I have given up all fancied joys, and I am searching for joys that endure. Will the man who has eaten poison and vomited it up, return to the tempting dish again? Will he who has escaped from the burning house voluntarily go back to the flames?"[1] His father could assure him of no release from sickness, death, decay; and it was this he sought.

It was from the recognised religious teachers, the Brahmans, he first sought direction. And it is important to observe the difficulties which chiefly perplexed him, and the point at which he felt their system to be weak. After living

[1] Beal's *Romantic Hist. of Buddha*, pp. 163–5.

for some days among a company of distinguished ascetics, and observing their practices, he begged to be allowed to question them, and receiving permission, he at once pierced to the heart of the matter. "Venerable sirs," he said, "I perceive that your system, although it promises the reward of heaven to certain persons, yet provides no means of *final* deliverance. You give up all, friends, relatives, and worldly delights, and suffer pain, that you may be born in heaven; not considering that after being thus born on high, you may in future years return and be born even in hell. In coveting to be born into heaven you forget that this very continuance involves the recurrence of the evil you now seek to escape from. So it is with men who when they come to die are filled with fear, and seek some happy state of birth, and through this very desire for life they doom themselves to return again to the inconstant state of life they have left. They do not consider the ever-recurring evil of future births. Coveting the joys of heaven, they do not consider that the very nature of the body, however pure and spiritual, involves the necessity of decay, and therefore of change." He also objects to the means which the Brahmans employed to gain their end. "If," he argued, "abstention from sufficient food is meritorious, the wild beasts, who are content with grass, ought to abound in merit; and the man who now suffers hardships ought, as a necessary consequence, to enjoy future happiness." Having thus disposed of asceticism, he as summarily exploded the practice of sacrifice. "How can the system which requires the infliction of misery on others be called a religious system? To seek a good by doing an evil is surely no safe plan. If a man, in worshipping the gods, sacrifices a sheep, and so does well, why should he not kill his child and so do better?"[1]

To these difficulties the Brahmans had little to reply. They could only say that it was by such methods all the ancient saints had attained felicity. These teachers make no mention of absorption into Brahma as the final deliverance; a circumstance which seems to indicate that this doctrine may have been helped to its complete development by the teachings of Buddha himself. Resorting in turn to the most celebrated of the Brahman sophists, Alara and Udra, he questioned them also, not as an itinerant disputant, of which in these days there were many, but as one who sought a physician, as a wanderer who had lost his way in the midst of a great solitary wild.[2] Nowhere could he find the object of his search—an escape from

[1] Beal, 157–9. [2] Ibid. 171.

the miseries and vanities of life into a condition from which no return to life and its troubles was possible. "I search," he said, "for that which is imperishable and permanent." He seemed to himself to be inextricably entangled in an existence in which everything was subject to the ceaseless rotation of decay, death, birth; decay, death, birth.

Failing to receive light from other men, he resolved to give himself to meditation, and retired for this purpose to the solitude of Uruvela. Here for six years he lived in the jungle with five other ascetics who attended him, already feeling that he was the greatest and most resolutely true teacher they had met. Even from this solitude the fame of his meditation and mortification, says the chronicle, "spread abroad like the sound of a great bell hung in the canopy of the skies." But the crisis was at hand. His physical strength gave way under his austerities. He swooned, and was thought to be dead. Recovering consciousness, it was only to fall into an agony of mental conflict, which the legends vainly strive to depict by a more than Miltonic picture of a battle between Buddha and Mara, armed with the most appalling instruments of destruction. Doubtless, in his state of physical inanition, the knowledge of his failure as yet to find deliverance opened the long-closed doors of his memory and flooded his spirit with regrets, and with the fond memories of his youthful life so utterly in contrast to the squalor and discomfort of the jungle. But gathering his energies for one supreme effort, he forced his mind, as the night wore through, to a strict sequence of thought, and as morning dawned the light he had so long sought broke upon him.

Such then was the process by which Siddartha painfully won his way to Buddhahood. Henceforth he was the Buddha, the Enlightened. At this point, however, the legendary histories, which speak of this eminence as one to which no other man could attain, are apt to make us forget that it was by a purely and confessedly human process he won his way to light, and that originally this title, the Buddha, can have meant nothing more than that he was recognised as a singularly successful thinker. The traditional accounts affirm that there had been many Buddhas before him, and that he expected his religion would last only for 5000 years, when some new Buddha would appear and supersede him. But the fact is that no historical person had borne this title before Sakya-muni. The Buddhaship was not a well-known vacancy waiting to be filled; it was an unknown office, an insignificant title, which now at last was lifted into exceptional, unique significance, by the importance of the person to whom at first it was almost casually given.

But no sooner did Sakya-muni become the Buddha than he was appalled at the laborious enterprise that awaited him in communicating his newly-attained light to all men.[1] He knew what it had cost himself to accept this light. He knew how men shrank from any teaching which forced truth into their convictions. Was it not hopeless to attempt the deliverance of men by such a system as his—a system involving change of character and entirely averse to all mere magical formulas or rites? But his compassion prevailed. For a time the struggle was severe, but soon we find him making his way to the great religious centre of Northern India with the resolve: "I now desire to turn the wheel of the excellent law; for this purpose am I going to that city of Benares, to give light to those enshrouded in darkness and to open the gate of immortality to men." At first he gained disciples rapidly. His princely appearance and bearing, the indubitable thoroughness of his often-tested self-abnegation and charity, his skill and persuasiveness and originality in teaching, and the reasonableness and purity of

[1] On the interposition of Brahma at this critical juncture, *vide* Bigandet, p. 105.

his doctrine, contributed to his success. He was soon in a position to attempt to "set rolling the royal chariot-wheel of a universal kingdom of right."[1] Calling his disciples about him, he conferred upon them the power hitherto reserved to himself, to admit members to the Buddhist Society, and sent them out in all directions to explain his religion to all. "Bhikshus," he said, "having myself escaped from all sorrows, I desire my own profit to redound to the good of others: there are yet a vast number of men enthralled by grief—for these we ought to have some care and compassion. Go now, therefore, and teach the most excellent law. Explain the beginning, the middle, and the end of the law to all men without exception; let everything respecting it be made publicly known, and be brought to the broad daylight."[2] During the remaining forty-five years of his life this was his regular procedure: while the rainy season lasted he and his apostles lived together under shelter, but as soon as it became possible for them to itinerate they scattered again in every direction, still turning the wheel of the law.

Buddha's own skill in teaching and his me-

[1] Rhys Davids in *Encyclopædia Brit.* p. 428. Cf. Beal, p. 244.

[2] Beal, p. 285. Bigandet, p. 122.

thod, as well as the missionary ardour of the new religion, are illustrated by the following incidents. Kisâgotami had been married early, and while still a girl gave birth to a son. When the boy was able to walk by himself he died. The young girl in her love for it carried the dead child clasped to her bosom, and went from house to house asking if any one could give her medicine for it. At length a wise man understanding her case thought with himself, "Alas! this Kisâgotami does not understand the law of death. I must comfort her." "My good girl," he said, "I cannot myself give medicine for your child, but I know of one who can." "Oh, tell me who that is," said she. "The Buddha can give you medicine; you must go to him." She went to Buddha, and doing homage to him, said, "Lord and master, do you know any medicine that will be good for my child?" "Yes," said the teacher; "I know of some. Get me a handful of mustard seed." But when the poor girl was hurrying away to procure it, he added, "I require mustard seed from a house where no son, husband, parent, or slave, has died." "Very good," said the girl, and went to ask for it, carrying still the dead child astride on her hip. The people said, "Here is mustard seed;" but when she asked, "Has there died a son, a husband, a parent, or a slave, in this house?" they replied, "Lady, what is this that you ask? the living are few, but the dead are many!" Then she went to other homes, but one said, "I have lost a son;" another, "I have lost my parents;" another, "I have lost my slave." At last, not being able to find a single house where no one had died, she began to think, "This is a heavy task that I am on." And as her mind cleared, she summoned up her resolution, left the dead child in a forest, and returned to Buddha. "Have you procured the mustard seed?" he asked. "I have not," she replied: "the people of the village told me, 'The living are few, but the dead are many.'" Then Buddha said, "You thought that you alone had lost a son: the law of death is that among all living creatures there is no permanence." Thus he cleared away her darkness of mind, helped her to contentment, and numbered her among his disciples.[1]

The other incident is told as follows:—A rich merchant, of the name of Purna, being converted to the teaching of Buddha by some of his companions on shipboard, resolved to forsake all and fix his residence with a neighbouring but savage tribe, in order to win them to the same religion. Buddha at first tried to dissuade him from so perilous an undertaking.

[1] Max Müller's Lecture on Nihilism, p. 16. Buddhaghosha's *Parables*, p. 98.

"The men of Sronaparanta, where you wish to fix your residence," he said, "are violent, cruel, passionate, fierce, and insolent. When these men address you in wicked, brutal, gross, and insulting language, when they storm at you and abuse you, what will you do, O Purna?"

"When they address me in wicked and insulting language, and abuse me," replied Purna, "this is what I will think. These men of Sronaparanta are certainly good and gentle men, who do not strike me either with their hands or with stones."

"But if they strike you, what will you think?"

"I will think them good and gentle, because they do not strike me with cudgels or with the sword."

"But what if they do strike you with the sword?"

"I will think them good and gentle, because they do not completely deprive me of life."

"But if they do deprive you of life, what then?"

"I will think the men of Sronaparanta good and gentle, for delivering me with so little pain from this body full of vileness."

"It is well, Purna," said Buddha; "with your perfect patience you may dwell among the

Sronaparantakas. Go thou, O Purna, thyself delivered, deliver others; thyself arrived at the other shore, help others thither; thyself comforted, comfort others; having attained complete Nirvana, guide others to it."

Thus commissioned, Purna betook himself to that desperate mission, and by his imperturbable patience, won the inhabitants to attend to his teaching.[1]

The zeal of these indomitable missionaries, who certainly have tamed many of the fiercest and rudest races upon the earth, was kindled at the undying flame of Buddha's own universal charity.[2] With his latest breath he continued to preach his gospel of deliverance. The last night of his life, when his friends would fain have secured him a little quiet, he overheard the voice of a well-known Brahman philosopher pleading to be allowed to ask him one or two questions. Buddha desired them to admit him, and addressed him in the following remarkable words: "This is not the time for discussions. To true wisdom there is only one way, the path is laid down in my law. Many have already followed it, and conquering the lust and pride

[1] St. Hilaire, *Le Bouddha et sa Religion*, pp. 95–97.

[2] "Le proselytisme lui-même n'est qu'un effet de ce sentiment de la bienveillance et de charité universelle qui anime le Buddha."—Burnouf, *Introd. à l'histoire du Buddhisme Indien*, p. 37.

and anger of their own hearts, have become free from ignorance and doubt and wrong belief, have entered the calm state of universal kindliness, and reached Nirvana even in this life. Except in my religion the twelve great disciples who practise the highest virtue, and stir up the world to free it from its indifference, are nowhere to be met with. O Subhadra, I do not speak to you of things I have not experienced. Since my twenty-ninth year have I striven after the supreme wisdom, and followed the path that leads to Nirvana."[1] Shortly after he said to his disciples: "Beloved, that which causes life, causes also decay and death. Never forget this, let your minds be filled with this truth. I called you to make it known to you." These were the last words of the Buddha.

Here, then, we have the essence of the salvation Buddha had to proclaim. *Life involves death.* Wherever there is life, decay must follow. In every form of existence there are already the germs of dissolution. To get rid of decay and its accompanying misery we must get quit of life; of life, not merely in this present world, but of life in every form. For in the Buddhist philosophy there is no such conception as a purely spiritual existence. He is a heretic who holds that man has a soul or

[1] Rhys Davids in *Encyc. Brit*, and Bigandet, p. 314.

permanent self separable from the body. Whatever is material is subject to change and dissolution, and there is no life which is not material. These are the postulates, the ultimate facts on which Buddhism proceeds. As long, therefore, as man *is*, he must be miserable. His only salvation is, not to be. There is no cure. The only escape from evil is escape from existence. The great problem comes to be, how to commit suicide; suicide not of that pitiful and delusive kind which rids a man of life in one particular form, but which rids him of existence in every form. The ultimate good to which the individual looks forward is annihilation; the consummation of all things which is to be prayed for and striven after is absolute universal nothing.

The two fixed ideas of Buddhism, as it appeared in the mind of its founder, are the materialistic nature of all existence and the doctrine of transmigration. These are the root principles out of which the system sprang.[1] The fundamental axioms of Buddhism, or, as they are technically called, the Four Great or Excellent Truths,[2] which constitute the discovery of Buddha, are these: 1. That in all

[1] Its Atheism, its Nihilism, are already contained in these root ideas.

[2] See Burnouf, pp. 299 and 629. Hardy's *Manual*, p. 496.

existence there is sorrow. 2. That all existence results from attachment to life, or desire. 3. That existence may be extinguished by extinguishing desire. 4. That desire may be extinguished by following the path to Nirvana. No doubt it will at once occur to you that the very foundation of this system is false. You will deny its first proposition, that in all existence there is sorrow. Some lives are wretched and a living death, but others are bright and full of joy. But from the materialistic point of view life is haunted with the shame and misery of the decay it carries in it, and from which there is no escape but into some other form of existence also destined to decay and corruption. Besides, the actual suffering and disappointment and sense of the vanity of life are so common, that any religious teacher who offers relief from these feelings is sure of much success. He was not a Buddhist who said, "There are moments of depression when we seem to feel still in need of some explanation why organic life should exist at all."

> "A life
> With large results so little rife,
> Though bearable, seems hardly worth
> This pomp of worlds, this pain of birth."[1]

---

[1] Andrew Wilson's *Abode of Snow*, p. 310. Comp. Shelley's stanzas written in dejection near Naples.

Possibly if we could detect the leading motives which have first disposed men to accept any religion, we should see that one of the most influential of these motives has always been the pressure or fear of misery, even of a physical or worldly kind. And it is also to be considered that in the countries where Buddhism has found its most permanent and influential acceptance life is difficult and precarious. In India there was, in addition to the natural shrinking from the known distresses of the present and the unknown calamities of the future, the loathing of existence which had been produced by the doctrine of transmigration.[1] So long as personal existence is retained the same risk attends every life as attends the present life. "The being who is still subject to birth," as one of the Buddhist writings reminds us, "may at one

[1] Some suggestive remarks on the difference between the Western optimist view of life, and the Eastern pessimist view, will be found in Sir Coomara Swamy's *Sutta Nipata*, Introd. p. xxviii. *et seq.* To the quotations there given we may add the apparently self-contradictory utterance of John Stuart Mill. "It seems to me not only possible, but probable, that in a higher, and, above all, in a happier condition of human life, not annihilation but immortality may be the burdensome idea; and that human nature, though pleased with the present, and by no means impatient to quit it, would find comfort and not sadness in the thought that it is not chained through eternity to a conscious existence, which it cannot be assured that it will always wish to preserve."

time sport in the garden of a déwa, and at another be cut to a thousand pieces in hell; at one time he may be Maha Brahma, and at another a degraded outcast; at one time he may eat the food of the déwas, and at another he may have molten lead poured down his throat; at one time he may sip nectar, and at another be made to drink blood; alternately he may become wild with pleasure, and then with pain; he may now be a king who can receive countless gems by the mere clapping of his hands, and now a mendicant, carrying a skull from door to door to gather alms."[1]

The personal upbringing and experience of Buddha had no doubt much to do with his depreciation of life. The side of it which had been represented to him as most valuable and attractive he had found to be utterly nauseating. And when he gazed on the ignominious decay of all that was outwardly bright, and put to himself the question whether there is actually any being who has not suffered or may not suffer, he may have erred in the form rather than in the substantial meaning of his answer. For, is there any moral existence which does not involve suffering?[2] The higher we ascend in the scale of being, the greater

[1] Hardy's *Manual*, p. 454.
[2] See Wilson's *Abode of Snow.*

capacity and readiness for suffering do we find. As we ascend, we find indeed that we are rising out of reach of that suffering which springs directly out of the moral wrong-doing of the sufferer, but we also find that, very much in the same proportion, there increases an inability to be happy while any other being is suffering, an incapacity to enjoy a solitary bliss, a craving for an equal distribution of suffering and blessedness, a will to share the one and communicate the other. Is not God God precisely because He shrinks from no responsibility His creatures lay upon Him; turns away from no suffering their sin or need entails; and does not rest until they are partakers of His blessedness? Buddha, therefore, was probably not so far wrong in his first proposition, that all existence involves sorrow, as in failing to consider that there are deeper evils than sorrow, and in refusing to lift his eyes to the eternal issues of things and take into his reckoning the permanent results of suffering on character.

But admitting that all existence is miserable, and that the great aim of man is to escape from misery, ought not consistent materialists to have relied upon death as their deliverer from life and its accompanying sorrow? Is not the dissipation of the bodily organism precisely the deliverance by extinction which men are supposed to long for? Far from it, says Buddha. When the body dies, there remains the aggregate moral result for good or evil of the life led in the body, and this moral result of the present life is the seed of a new existence. Every form of life now in existence, and indeed every form of existence animate or inanimate, is the result of previously existing things, and especially of the moral value of these previously existing things; so all that now exists will by its moral character reproduce and determine the next generation of existences. This is the Buddhist doctrine of Karma. Karma means "act;" and the doctrine of karma is that a man's condition in this present life is the consequence of his actions in a previous state, and that he determines by his actions in this life what his future condition will be. Until a man's karma is satisfied, until he has entirely exhausted the consequences of his past actions, he must continue to be reborn in one form or another. A young Brahman came to Gautama and said: "From some cause or other mankind receive existence; but there are some persons who are exalted, others who are mean; some who die young, others who live to a great age; some who suffer from various diseases, others who have no sickness until they die; . . . some who are of mean birth, others who belong to the highest castes. What is the cause of these differences? What is it that appoints or controls these discrepancies?" To which Buddha replied: "All sentient beings have their own individual karma, or the most essential property of all beings is their karma; karma comes by inheritance not from parentage but from previous births; karma is the cause of all good and evil. . . . It is the difference in the karma that causes the difference in the lot of men, so that some are mean and others are exalted, some are miserable and others happy."[1] From this law Gautama himself was not exempt, but declared that he obtained the Buddhaship "neither by his own inherent power nor by the assistance of the déwas, but by the meritorious karma of previous births."[2] Slowly had he won his way to this high position, having passed through every form of life—being born as a bird, as a stag, as an elephant, even as a tree or plant; having experienced every rank and condition of human life by successive births into each, and only after exhausting this long probation and rising to increasing altitudes of purity and self-sacrifice, being born at last into the heaven from which Buddhas descend to earth.

Though quite untenable, and not even professing to justify itself to reason, there is much

[1] Hardy, pp. 445, 6. [2] Ibid. p. 448.

that is commendable and attractive in this theory of karma. If it does not so much as attempt to explain the origin of the universe, it at least points to a moral and not a physical necessity as regulating the amount of life and the nature of life in all worlds. As it is the karma of the individual which necessitates his being born again and again until he can attain Nirvana, so it is "by the aggregate karma of the various orders of living beings that the present worlds were brought into existence."[1] Buddhism declines to say anything about the originating of karma, or what it was which brought the first living beings into existence before any karma existed; but confining itself to the present actual world, it refuses to rest the condition of man, his miseries and his existence, on anything but a moral foundation. For the same reason it refused to recognise a personal Creator, because that would be to rest the blame of human existence on the wrong shoulders, and charge a Creator with all the actual misery exhibited wherever life is seen. And undoubtedly if it makes individuals feel responsible for all the ills that befall them, it acts also as a powerful incentive to virtue. The man who believes that every evil act will inevitably have its consequence, and that as he sows he shall reap;

[1] Hardy, p. 396.

the man who is convinced that sloth, selfishness, fraud, or lust, in this life, will necessitate his being born at death into the terrible Buddhist hell[1] or into some vile crawling creature, and that from that condition he can only slowly and laboriously win his way by righteous living back into his present state; the man who accepts such a doctrine has at least one powerful inducement to virtue.

It is obvious that were such a doctrine preached to Europeans it would at once be met by the assertion, that as we have no consciousness of any life prior to this, in which we sowed what now we are reaping, so we shall have no remembrance of our present selves in any future state. There is no continuity of personal identity. It is not really I who am to be reborn, but another person who is to be born and bear my guilt or enjoy my merit. When I die, there remains only my karma, and this karma of mine necessitates the birth of a man or a beast; but in this man or beast there will be no consciousness of identity with me, nor will my consciousness be

[1] Adulterers, after being boiled for immense periods in the lowest hell, are transferred into the Lohakumbha hell-pot, the bottom of which they reach in 30,000 years. The same time is spent in coming up to the surface; and so on. Well may they say: "To the foolish, who know not the law of the righteous, the life to come is long."—Buddhaghosha's *Parables*, p. 132.

continued in that life of retribution. The sin is punished, but not the sinner. Buddhism, denying, as it did, the immateriality of the soul, had this objection in view at a very early period, and met it by the analogical reasoning which was so much in vogue. The king Milinda, in the course of conversation with Nagasena, the Buddhist sage, criticises the doctrine of karma thus: "If the *same* man is not again produced, that being at least is delivered from the consequences of sinful action."[1] To which Nagasena replies, "How so? If there be *no* future birth there is deliverance; but if there be a future birth, deliverance does not necessarily follow. Thus a man steals a number of mangos, and takes them away; but he is seized by the owner, who brings him before the king, and says, 'Sire, this man has stolen my mangos.' But the robber replies, 'I have not stolen his mangos; the mango he set in the ground was one, these mangos are other and different.' Will this plea be sustained? Or a man while eating his food allows his lamp to flare up and set fire to the thatch, and, the flame extending, the whole village is burned. But when the villagers seize him, he says, 'Good people, I did not burn your village; the flame that I kindled was one, but the flame

[1] Hardy's *Manual*, p. 429.

that burned your village was another.' Will they listen to him?"

If, then, all life is a misery, and if the bodily death of the individual leaves still a germ which will produce a renewal of life and of misery, how is this germ to be got rid of? The answer is given in a standard Buddhist writing in the following explicit terms:[1] "What are the four sublime truths? Sorrow, the production of sorrow, the extinction of sorrow, the path which conducts to the extinction of sorrow. What is the sorrow which is the first great truth? It is birth, old age, disease, death; it is being bound to what you hate and separated from what you love; it is powerlessness to obtain what you desire and seek. What is the production of sorrow? It is the ceaseless, ever-recurring desire, accompanied by pleasure and passion, to find satisfaction in one thing or other. What is the extinction of sorrow? It is the complete destruction of this ever-recurring desire; it is detachment from this desire—its abandonment, extinction, annihilation; it is the perfect renunciation of this desire. And what is the path which conducts to this? It is the path which is laid down by these eight things: right views, right will, right effort, right action, right living, right

[1] Burnouf's *Introd.* p. 629.

speech, right thought, and right meditation." Desire, in short, is the root-evil which must be destroyed. The thirst for life and its short-lived empty pleasures must be got rid of. The ignorance which betrays men, causing them always to renew their belief in the satisfying nature of life, must be dispelled. They must learn to see things as they are, and to understand that as man never is, so never will he be blessed, save by ceasing to be. Ignorance and desire, these are man's disease; ignorance which cannot see the impermanence and vanity of all things; desire which attaches man to life, and carries him, like the crow on the elephant's carcase, down the river, till he finds himself seated on a skeleton picked clean, and hopelessly lost in mid-ocean. The suppression of desire, therefore, by the help of wisdom, is the Buddhist means of salvation. Here is the doctrine in Sakya-muni's own words. "Existence is a tree; the merit or demerit of the actions of men is the fruit of that tree and the seed of future trees; death is the withering away of the old tree from which the others have sprung; wisdom and virtue take away the germinating faculty, so that when the tree dies there is no reproduction. This is Nirvana."[1] Or, as the same doctrine is taught

[1] Wilson, ii. 364.

in another Buddhist writing: "The heart, scrupulously avoiding all idle dissipation, diligently applying itself to the holy law of Buddha, letting go all lust and consequent disappointment, fixed and unchangeable, enters on Nirvana."[1]

But it must not be supposed that the mere conquest of sensuality, nor even the eradication of all malevolent passion, is enough to lift the disciple into Nirvana. The highest condition, the Buddhist's perfect blessedness, is attained only by those who have so absolutely conquered self that they do not even desire continued existence for themselves, but have given up their hold of everything, and have thus attained perfect inward peace and charity. It is this sublimated Stoicism, this condition of perfect self-renunciation, which constitutes the Buddhist Nirvana, and which destroys the possibility of any future existence. Thus, when a young Bramatchari asked Buddha to explain to him his secret, he replied, "Illustrious youth, if a man let go his hold on the world so as to store up no further karma, this man will understand the character of permanence and of non-permanence." Similarly to another inquirer he says, "When the world, weary of sorrow, turns away and separates itself from the cause

[1] Beal's *Buddhist Scriptures*, p. 159.

of all this sorrow, then, by this voluntary rejection of it, there remains that which I call 'the true self.'"[1]

Nirvana, then, is the moral condition which accompanies the eradication of self-will, self-assertion, self-seeking, self-pleasing. And had this been the ultimate aim of Buddhism, nothing could have been worthier of human effort. But this moral self-renunciation is only a means to the great end of annihilation, extinction of self in every sense. Self is to be renounced, not that man may come into a loving concord with the will of God and with every living creature, but that he may himself escape the misery which inevitably accompanies all existence. The moral condition of Nirvana is attained in order that at death there may be no re-birth. The oil is withdrawn and the flame dies out, so that no other wick can be lit from it. Unconsciously it would, no doubt, be the moral attainment which satisfied high-minded Buddhists; but theoretically the moral attainment is not the ultimate end in view, but only the means by which the man attains to non-existence. He reaches the highest development, not to become serviceable to the world

[1] Beal's *Buddhist Scrip.* pp. 180, 185. An instructive comparison of the system of Schopenhauer with that of Buddha will be found in Helen Zimmern's *Arthur Schopenhauer.* c. x.

at large, but to pass away into nothingness. "He that hateth his life in this world, shall keep it unto life eternal"—that is the well-balanced, far-seeing, quiet enunciation of the real law of existence; but the Buddhist Nirvana is a travestie of this, and magnificent as is the conception of man's highest moral state, it is stultified by the end for which it is to be attained.

And thus, though the framework of the Buddhist ethic is beautiful and all but perfect, the moving spirit of it is radically selfish. It not only professedly excludes all consideration of a higher will than a man's own, but it also excludes all idea of duty. It takes its departure from man's sense of misery, not from his sense of sin; it builds its well-proportioned and exquisitely-chiselled temple not on conscience, but on man's craving for happiness; and its ultimate aim is not to free men from inward evil, but to emancipate them from misery, that is, from existence. And therefore, while the admirable purity and elevation of its moral teaching must have found a hopeful response in many a soul, it has signally failed in moving the multitude. It has in it the makings of the purest moral system men have ever developed, but it lacks the two elements which are chiefly needed in any system which is to be extensively efficacious among men: it lacks the appeal to conscience which furnishes the steady support of a sense of duty, and it lacks the idea of a personal God which calls out the still stronger, if as yet less constant, principles of love and hope.

But not only does Buddhism show us how hopeless it is to endeavour to communicate to nations a high morality apart from a pure religious faith, it also shows us that the purest natural instincts point to the same morality which our religion teaches. It gives us the proof that in bidding us extinguish self, our Lord commands that which the truest human wisdom working in a purely human interest itself dictates.

The most competent living authority on Buddhism, Mr. Rhys Davids, has elaborated a theory which, though it owes, I think, more to his own elevated moral sentiment than to Buddhist principles, yet deserves to be noticed, both on account of its intrinsic beauty and in deference to its originator. It is a theory in which the Comtists will recognise that Buddhism has anticipated them not only in their materialism and agnosticism, but also in their worship of humanity and sacrifice of the individual to the race. For the theory is this: that the Buddhist, in seeking Nirvana, knows that this involves his own personal extinction, but is upheld by the hope that he will thus lessen the sum of human misery. By destroying his karma, by annihilating this seed of a new existence, he withdraws one individual life from the sum of beings who are going the weary round of ever-recurring births. "The true Buddhist saint does not stain the purity of his self-denial by lusting after a positive happiness which he himself is to enjoy hereafter. His consciousness will cease to feel, but his virtue will live and work out its full effect in the decrease of the sum of the misery of sentient beings."[1] He helps forward the universe to its goal of non-existence. He leaves behind him no inheritance of misery. He himself ceases to be, and no one takes his place; there is one unit the less to live and to suffer. This is the Buddhist analogue to the Positivist offset to personal annihilation so winningly presented by George Eliot:—

"O may I join the choir invisible
Of those immortal dead who live again
In minds made better by their presence: live
In pulses stirred to generosity,
In deeds of daring rectitude, in scorn
For miserable aims that end with self,
In thoughts sublime that pierce the nightlike stars,

[1] *Contemporary Review*, January, 1877.

And with their mild persistence urge man's search
To vaster issues. . . .
This is life to come."[1]

Certainly it is competent to a Buddhist to cherish this desire for the universal good, and the religion out of which such thoughts can be even logically evolved is thereby proved to be worthy of earnest study and of much consideration. Neither ought it to be overlooked that, with the exception of Christianity, no religion has laid such stress upon the grace of universal charity as Buddhism lays. Buddha himself said, "A man who foolishly does me wrong, I will return to him the protection of my ungrudging love; the more evil comes from him the more good shall go from me." "A wicked man who reproaches a virtuous one is like one who looks up and spits at heaven; the spittle soils not the heaven, but comes back and defiles his own face." Again, in a very remarkable passage, "To feed crowds by the hundred is not to be compared to the act of feeding one really good man; to feed good men by the thousand is not to be compared to the act of feeding one lay-disciple;" and so on through all the ranks of Buddhist saintship, till we come to the

[1] To the same purpose Mr. John Morley has consecrated some of the most eloquent passages in the English language.

highest: "'To feed Pratyêka Buddhas by the thousand myriad is not like feeding one Buddha, and learning to pray to him *from a desire to save all living creatures.* To feed one good man, however, is of infinitely greater merit than attending to questions about heaven and earth, spirits and demons, such as occupy ordinary men. These matters are not to be compared to the religious duties we owe to our parents. Our parents are very Divine."[1] And, as here hinted, it is not only love to parents and Buddhists that is enjoined, but universal charity; love for all living beings, and that of the most substantial kind. "As a mother, even at the risk of her own life, protects her son, her only son, so let there be good-will without measure among all beings. Let good-will without measure—unhindered love and friendliness—prevail in the whole world, above, below, around." But although Buddha himself practised this universal charity and engaged in his search after truth for the world's sake as well as for his own, there is no evidence that he desired extinction in order to lessen the sum of misery and not rather to terminate his own. Indeed the words in which Buddha exultantly celebrated the dawn of light in his mind imply that his escape from the danger of re-birth was a subject of congratula-

[1] Beal's *Bud. Scrip.* pp. 193, 4.

tion exclusively to himself. "Through various transmigrations have I passed, always vainly seeking to discover the builder of my tabernacle. Painful are repeated transmigrations. But now, O builder, thou art discovered. Never shalt thou build me another house. Thy frames are broken, thy ridge-pole shattered. To Nirwana my mind is gone. I have attained to the extinction of desire."[1]

Buddhism stands in no need of any doubtfully imported merit. It has a genuine and obvious merit of its own. It proclaims the fundamental truth that men obtain deliverance from their evil destiny and enter into blessedness only when they attain to perfect life and character. No sooner was this salvation proclaimed, than the vast sacerdotal system of India, with its ritual and its caste, was felt to be a useless encumbrance. Buddha did not make war upon caste, but as he had discovered salvation by considering the nature of man, and as his salvation was equally applicable to all men, caste lost its religious character wherever Buddhism gained ascendency. Buddhism has thus the merit of anticipating Christianity in two of its most striking features—its universalism and its ethical character. *All* men may be saved, and they are saved, not at all by outward rites or

[1] Various versions given in Hardy's *Manual*, pp. 180, 1.

mechanical performances, but by themselves being emancipated from inward evil.

Practically, however, Buddhism must be admitted to have been to a large extent a failure. In no country has it rooted itself more firmly than in Mongolia, and here, while its high morality is ignored, the germs of evil which the system carried in it have found luxuriant development. From the first, Buddhism reserved its highest blessings for the man of contemplation, who could pass through the world as the stick floats down the river—unattracted to either bank. Its fundamental principles also discouraged the increase of population. If life could only be miserable, the celibate has a higher degree than the married man. So that although a man may be a good Buddhist while supporting a family by ordinary business in the world, the actual result of the system is, that in those countries where its influence is most felt not less than one-third of the male population become lamas or monks. In one monastery there are said to be as many as thirty thousand lamas, and several others throughout Tibet and Mongolia number their inmates by thousands. It so happens that in some districts this restriction of population is a boon, owing to the sterility of the soil and the difficulty of emigration. Buddhism and polyandry are evils that work for good. But the withdrawal of so large a part of the population from productive labour, and their exemption from taxes, as well as the constant anxiety produced in the empire of China[1] by so large a body of men contiguous to their border, and ready to act at the word of the Dalai Lama, seriously retard the civilization of these countries. Lamaism, while it is the strength of the Buddhist religion, is, according to the most recent explorer, "the most frightful curse" of Mongolia.[2] Cruelty and immorality, the two vices against which primitive Buddhism most emphatically declared itself, are here common and unopposed. The Buddhist who before sitting down will brush his seat lest he crush an insect, will slaughter his prisoners in cold blood; and the religion which originally laid such stress upon meditation and wisdom, is now represented, if we except Burmah, by a priesthood that is disgracefully ignorant.

All religions undergo rapid and important alterations. The difference between any religion as it exists in the actual popular acceptation of it, and the same religion as it existed in the mind of its founder, is generally marked and

[1] Wilson, ii. 373. Wilson's *Abode of Snow*, p. 224, &c. Prejevalsky's *Mongolia*, i. 76.

[2] Prejevalsky, i. 80.

significant. Every religion is modified by the racial characteristics of the nations among whom it finds acceptance. It is dragged down to the comprehension and forced into the forms of thought of a half-educated people, and it is compelled to assume a dress which effectually disguises and hampers it. It is difficult to identify the dialect of Somersetshire and that of Berwickshire as the same language; but it is still more difficult to detect any close relationship between the superstitious and idolatrous religion of the Northern Buddhists and the original system of Buddha. No religion, indeed, not even Christianity, has suffered such alteration at the hands of its devotees as Buddhism has suffered.

In two particulars only can this alteration be here noted. It might have been expected that if the original ritual of Buddhism was too scant for the popular mind, it would at least preserve its adherents from formalism. The actual result is the very opposite. The perfunctory performance of religious rites and the necessarily accompanying superstition have attained gigantic proportions in Buddhist countries. It is true that the ritual of the Parsees, as well as the most sacred canon of the Hindus, are in a language not understood by the priests themselves, while the breviary of the Roman Catholics is in a language not understood by the people; but among the Buddhists the prayer which may be said to be their Paternoster, and which is repeated many times a day by millions of lips, is wholly unintelligible both to priests and to people. Intelligent travellers have tried in vain to discover the meaning of the mystical words, "Om mani padme hum;" and competent scholars disagree as to their origin and interpretation;[1] and yet these are the first syllables which the child is taught to pronounce, and the last breath of the dying Buddhist is shaped into these unintelligible but saving words. "The wanderer," we are told, "murmurs them on his way, the herdsman beside his cattle, the matron at her household tasks, the monk in all the stages of contemplation: they form at once a cry of battle and a shout of victory. They are to be read wherever the Lama Church has spread, upon banners, upon rocks, upon trees, upon walls, upon monuments of stone, upon household utensils, upon human skulls and skeletons."[2] A cry of distress or a sigh of relief or confidence need not be articulate in order to be both genuine and intelligible to the person

[1] A facsimile of this prayer is given by Schlagintweit, *Buddhism in Tibet*, p. 120. The interpretation which has found greatest acceptance is: "O the jewel in the lotus. Amen." Wilson thinks it means, "Glory to Manipadme."

[2] Heeley and Koeppen, quoted by Prejevalsky, i. 282.

to whom it is uttered; and it ought not to be denied that through these sacred words many a true and profound emotion has found expression. To pray inarticulately is at all events better than not to pray at all. But the charge of formalism is made good when another feature of Buddhist prayer is adduced. Praying by proxy is common in all religions, but praying by machinery is apparently the invention of Buddhism. These mysterious words, "Om mani padme hum," are written or printed many times over on long scrolls of paper, which are wound within a small brass cylinder. This cylinder rotates upon an axis, and as often as it is set spinning so many prayers are said. These cylinders are carried by the lamas, who keep them spinning as they converse with you; they are fixed in the walls of houses, and as often as any of the family passes, another turn is given to the wheel; they are also provided with fans and set on the tops of houses, where the wind keeps them moving, or in a stream, which drives the praying mill for behoof of the community.

The most significant change, however, which has passed upon Buddhism is its abandonment of atheism. In speaking of Buddhism as an atheistic religion, it is essential to distinguish between the original and consistent system and the aftergrowth which sprang from the root of human instinct and national prepossession. Buddha himself makes no recognition of a personal God, but this creed was found too abstract and impersonal for popular acceptance, and the religious instincts of the masses introduced various forms of quasi-divine worship.

That the original system of Buddha was atheistic is unquestionable. There is a conversation recorded in which Sakya-muni interrogates Alara, the wisest of the Brahmans, as to the existence of an Isvara or Supreme God who alone deserves worship. Alara mentions the Great Brahma as such a Being. But, objects Buddha, what becomes of him at the end of the kalpa, when this present heaven and earth are entirely burnt up and destroyed—where then is your Creator? Again, Buddha argues that if all things had been created by Isvara, then all things must have been good, and there could have been no possibility of evil; there could have been no causes of sorrow, neither could there have been any difficulties of belief; this very question regarding the existence of Isvara could have found no place, but all men would have known him as their Father—an argument which in other religions also has led men to abandon monotheism.

Alara has indeed the best of the discussion when he presses Buddha regarding the origin of the world and man, but as intelligent Buddhists in our own day evade this difficulty by declaring it to be a profitless inquiry, so Buddha himself at this point disclaimed the character of a disputant, and declared himself to be speaking as one "who participates in the great mass of evil which exists, and who seeks only a physician."[1]

These utterances are sufficiently explicit. It is also obvious that the fundamental principles of Buddhism are inconsistent with theism. These principles do not necessitate nor invite to the recognition of any beings which are not radically of the same nature as man, and which are not exposed to the same risks as he. It agrees better, as one of our best authorities affirms, with the genius of the system propounded by Gautama "to suppose that, like other sceptics, he believed in neither angel nor demon, than to imagine that the accounts of the déwas and other supernatural beings we meet with in works called Buddhistical were known at its first promulgation."[2]

But supernaturalism asserted itself immediately, and the various polytheists who accepted Buddhism compensated themselves for the de-

[1] Beal's *Romantic Hist.* p. 173. Alabaster's *Wheel of the Law*, passim. Hardy's *Manual*, p. 375.

[2] Hardy, pp. 40, 41.

privation of their ancestral gods by setting Buddha above them, and paying him a similar worship. Brahma and Indra were repudiated as supreme gods; but Brahma is represented as paying religious honours to the discarded robe of Sakya-muni, while Indra descends from the heaven of the thirty-three gods to secure the dish from which the Buddha had eaten, and to set it up as an object of worship in his own heavenly abode.

Universally among Buddhists attributes which are recognised as divine are attributed to Buddha, especially the attributes of supremacy and omniscience. He is "the joy of the whole world; the helper of the helpless; the déwa of déwas; the brahma of brahmas; the very compassionate; more powerful than the most powerful; able to bestow Nirvana on him who only softly pronounces his name, or gives in his name a few grains of rice. The eye cannot see anything, the ear cannot hear anything, nor the mind think of anything more excellent or more worthy of regard than Buddha."[1] Of all personal beings Buddha is the highest.

It may indeed be thought[2] that this does not amount to deification. And this is true so far as regards instructed Buddhists; but it would appear that the common people in Nepaul wor-

[1] Hardy, p. 360. [2] St. Hilaire, p. 168.

ship one Supreme Buddha, called Adi-Buddha, relying upon him for protection and salvation, and "treating him to all practical intents and purposes as if he were the highest God, a personal being of unlimited wisdom, goodness, and power, the very creator and sustainer of the world."[1]

But besides Buddha himself there are others to whom worship is paid, although possibly only of that lower kind which a devout Romanist pays to the saints. The heroes and benefactors of the Buddhist Church could readily fill a Comtist calendar, and are surrounded with a legendary halo which lifts them as much above the ordinary level of humanity as demigods and saints are exalted by the mythologies of Greece or the Acta Sanctorum of more modern times. And it is significant that the ancient atheism as well as the modern was compelled to deify humanity, that the individual might at least have the satisfaction of looking up to and trusting in something higher than himself. Images of these saints profusely adorn or disfigure the Buddhist temples. Conspicuous among them, however, are images of the Buddhist Trinity, Buddha, Dharma, and Sangha. Tradition tells us that when Buddha felt himself dying he called Ananda to him, and said, "Ananda, when

[1] Eitel's *Lectures*, p. 117.

I am gone you must not think there is no Buddha; the discourses I have delivered and the precepts I have enjoined [*i.e.*, Dharma] must be my successor and representative, and be to you as Buddha." And among the seven imperishable precepts he gave to his disciples, the first in order was "to keep assemblies" [Sangha]. From the earliest times admission was given to the Buddhist Church on the repetition of the confession, "I take refuge in Buddha, Dharma, and Sangha;" and with its wonderful gift for personification, the Eastern mind has elevated these three to a quasi-divine rank.

But by far the most remarkable development of Buddhist belief and worship belongs to the mystical period of its history. During this period Amitabha, the Eternal, originally a title of Buddha, began to be worshipped by the Chinese as the compassionate and loving Father of men, or as the "universal Self." But as "Self" manifests itself by Speech, Speech was regarded as the Son or manifestation of the Eternal Self, and was adored under the name of Avalokiteshwara, the manifested God.[1] This Divinity, who has "a thousand arms and a thousand eyes and a merciful heart," and who has bound himself by an oath "to save completely

[1]Beal's *Buddhist Scrip.* p. 374.

all that breathes," is accepted by many millions as the invisible head of the present Buddhist Church, and is popularly believed to listen with compassion to the prayers of all in distress, to assist in the propagation of the faith, and to give entrance into the heavenly Paradise which has superseded the blank Nirvana in the hopes of the multitude.

IV.

THE PERFECT RELIGION.

"*On its historical side, Christianity will hover in the air so long as all religions are not recognised in their* essential *relation to it, as negative or positive preparations for it.*" DORNER.

"*The glory of Christianity is not to be as unlike other religions as possible, but to be their perfection and fulfilment.*" JOWETT.

"*Pour condamner le Christianisme, il faut ne pas le comprendre.*" ST. HILAIRE.

IV.

ONE cannot fail to notice in the literature of the day a tendency more or less pronounced to put all religions, including the Christian, more nearly on one level, and especially to deal with them as if they were all alike outgrowths from the same root, man's religious faculty. This tendency has been stimulated by the comparative method of studying religions, which has brought to light the large number of resemblances existing in the various religions of the world, but which has as yet been backward in detecting, analysing, and defining essential distinctions. Archæological researches have discovered the common origin of many customs, traditions, and beliefs, now found in countries widely separated from one another. Historical knowledge has done much to show us the processes by which a rude and barbarous tribe may be developed into a refined and highly civilised nation; and as we see how such a system as our own civil constitution has been gradually elaborated out of the summary despotism of a tribal chief, the thought cannot but occur to us, May not the most perfectly elaborated religious system have also grown up without other aids than those which are given in human nature and in history governed solely by natural laws? As man was created with a faculty of speech, and with instincts and emotions prompting him to communicate with his fellows, but was not endowed with any actual language, may not his religious equipment have been of a similar kind? As he was certain to create for himself a language sufficient for his occasions, and competent to bring him effectually into all needed communication with his fellow-men, was it not enough that he possessed also a religious faculty enabling him to hold fellowship with God, and sure to find utterance for itself in ways not unpleasing nor unintelligible to Him who had implanted the faculty?

Certainly this is a suggestion much more worthy of discussion than the theories which found acceptance last century, to the effect that religions were the product of fear or the contrivances of priests. It is now generally agreed that religion is universal; and that, being universal, it is necessary; that the faculty for holding intercourse with the unseen and supernatural is an essential part of human nature.[1] From

[1] See Fairbairn's *Studies*, p. 303.

man's universal use of some form of food, we conclude that food is necessary, and that man's power of assimilating it is an essential part of his nature. Similarly, when we find that, with some inconsiderable exceptions, all men have some form or other of religion, we conclude that the religious faculty is essential to human nature, and will always find for itself some expression. To quote the words of M. Rénan, who will not be suspected of undue bias in the matter: "Is religion destined to die away like the popular fallacies concerning magic, sorcery, and ghosts? By no means. Religion is not a popular fallacy: it is a great and intuitive truth, felt and expressed by the people. All the symbols which serve to give shape to the religious sentiment are imperfect, and their fate is to be one after the other rejected. But nothing is more remote from the truth than the dream of those who seek to imagine a perfected humanity without religion. The contrary idea is the truth. The effect of progress in humanity will not destroy or weaken religion, but will develop and increase it."[1] Indeed even Cicero foresaw that time would only serve to purify religion and render it more stable. "We see," he says, "that imaginations and mere opinions wear out and disappear. Who now believes in the cen-

[1] Rénan, *The Apostles* (E. T.), pp. 286, 7.

taur or chimæra? What old woman is so silly as to trouble herself nowadays with the horrors of hell, which once formed a part of every one's creed? For time destroys the fabrications of opinion, but confirms the decisions of nature. And therefore, both in our own and other countries, the worship of the gods and the sanctities of religions grow daily stronger and purer."[1] "More and more," says another inquirer into this subject, "as they become better known to us, the original forms of all religions are seen to fall under the category of nature and less under that of mind or free will. Religions, like languages, are inherent in all men everywhere, having a close sympathy or connection with political and family life. It would be a shallow and imaginary explanation of them that they are corruptions of some primeval revelation, or impostures framed by the persuasive arts of magicians or priests."[2]

Religion, then, must be defined as that which satisfies this faculty for dealing with the supernatural. The etymological definition of Lactantius, which declares religion to be that by which we are connected with or bound to God, whether right or wrong as etymology, is true as a definition. Newman's definition is also careful and

[1] *De Nat. Deor.* ii. 2.

[2] Jowett, *St. Paul's Epistles*, ii. 437.

exact: "What is religion but the system of relations subsisting between us and a supreme Power?"[1] More recently it has been said[2] that religion is "man's belief in a being or beings mightier than himself and inaccessible to his senses, but not indifferent to his sentiments and actions, with the feelings and practices which flow from such a belief." That which is common to all religions is the effort they make to bring man into harmony with the supernatural, with that which he cannot control by physical force. And it may be added that, if we define religion from that which is found to be common to all religions, it is the effort to come into satisfactory relations with some *personal* being or beings in whom the supernatural centres. In presence of much of the current philosophy it is indeed a great assumption we make when we assume that personality is a higher form of existence than impersonality. But we are now only accepting what the religions of the world teach us, and unquestionably they teach us nothing more distinctly than this, that the religious faculty in man considers personality the true form of the supernatural. Brahmanism has attempted to substitute for a personal God a being universally diffused and constituting all forms of life, but the unsophisticated cravings

[1] *Univ. Ser.* p. 19.

[2] Flint's *Baird Lect.* Lect. ii.

of the Hindus demand personal objects of worship and trust. Buddhism began its career without taking account of God at all, but has only succeeded thereby in giving birth to a peculiarly degraded polytheism.

If religion, then, be the medium of communication between God and men, that religion is the best which most perfectly brings God and man together. In other words, the best religion must furnish us with the true idea of God, and must enable us to come into the most perfect harmony with Him that is possible. No sooner, then, is the definition of religion clearly before the mind, than it condemns as imperfect many forms of religion which have been largely adhered to. All religions which propose to bring men into harmony with God by rites and merely substitutionary sacrifices, all religions which furnish men with the means of appeasing an angry God but with no means of loving Him, must be dismissed as unsatisfying. Proof is afforded that such religions do not satisfy the healthiest religious cravings, by the fact that alongside of sacerdotalism there has commonly grown up a development of mysticism or theosophic speculation.[1] This is the effort of nature to find a more real approach to God than priestly rites afford.

[1] See this finely illustrated in Fairbairn's *Studies*, p. 143.

Again, no sooner do we clearly see what religion is than we are at once compelled to dismiss certain criterions which have sometimes been applied to distinguish Christianity from other religions. We cannot, *e.g.*, cite in proof of the superiority of Christianity the fact that for defence of its truth, and in reliance upon it, many suffered martyrdom. Every religion has had its victims. The martyrs of Babism have left as touching memorials of their constancy as those we read in the annals of the Christian Church. The freeness and confidence with which women and girls submitted to torture or faced the beasts in the amphitheatres convinced observant spectators that in the religion for which they died there was certainly something strengthening, and probably something true. Many were moved in precisely the same way as Justin, who himself subsequently laid down his life for his religion. "I myself," he says, "while a Platonist heard the Christians evil spoken of, but when I saw them fearless in regard to death and all else that men count terrible, I began to see that they could not possibly be wicked sensualists." That is to say, martyrdom may provoke inquiry, but cannot prove the truth of a religion. Neither can success be accepted as a criterion. To use the words of John Henry Newman, "It is indeed by no means clear that Christianity has at any time been of any great spiritual advantage *to the world at large*. . . . The true light of the world offends more men than it attracts; and its divine origin is shown, not in its marked effects on the mass of mankind, but in its surprising power of elevating the moral character where it is received in spirit and in truth."[1] We need not expect, therefore, to find that we can rank religions in proportion to the number of their adherents.

In short, we must judge of the actual religions of the world by their relative competency to give men the highest idea of God, and to bring men into the profoundest harmony with Him.

I.—That religion is the best which gives us the highest idea of God; and that idea of God is the highest which is most satisfying to the intellect, most educating to the conscience, most quickening to the spirit, and, therefore, most influential on the conduct. We would say that that religion is the *true* religion which gives us the *true* idea of God; but we are proceeding by the method of comparing actual religions one with another, and must therefore, for the present, content ourselves with saying that, in comparison with other religions, that is the *best* which gives us the highest idea of God. Now, it were affectation to profess any difficulty at

[1] *University Sermons*, p. 40.

this point. It is not pretended by any writers whose thoughts on this subject have been accepted as a distinct development of religious thought in the country, that there is any higher or worthier idea of God to be found in any religion than in Christianity. Nay, it is not pretended that there is any higher or worthier idea of God present to the mind of the most disciplined or spiritual thinker than that which was conveyed by Christ. No such idea has been published. The religion of Christ has actually conveyed to the world its best idea of God. It is this idea which has satisfied the most advanced races, and the most religious natures among these races. And it has satisfied them by the combination which it alone presents of infinite exaltation and infinite lowliness, of absolute holiness and inexhaustible love.

Now, if we inquire what lay at the root of this superiority of the Christian idea of God, the first explanation we meet with is that this was the idea given by God Himself. Other ideas of God fall short, and the human spirit grows past them; but this idea remains unsurpassed, for the simple reason that while the former embody men's thoughts about God, the latter embodies God's revelation of Himself. No explanation could be more satisfactory or better fit the facts; but is it true? I cannot be expected to bring before you what is commonly and justly adduced in proof of a revelation, but may be allowed to pursue a single line of inquiry suggested by the question, Have we any means of determining whether in the one case we have only men's thoughts about God, and in the other a revelation by God Himself? I think we have. And although every revelation will always be its own best evidence to those who are mentally and spiritually in its own plane, it may yet be worth while to offer that which bears some resemblance, not indeed to demonstration, but to scientific proof of a revelation.[1]

Scientific inquiry, if it has not been able to measure the idea of revelation all round, and explain to us its method, has at least enabled us to approximate to a definition of it. If we find any race in possession of an idea, the roots of which we cannot trace to any inquiry on their part or to any contact with other races, we may fairly say that this is a revelation; supposing always that this idea is found to be true, and is concerned with matters supernatural. The line can, apparently, be drawn between the outcome of unassisted human thought

[1] As Rothe says: "The existence of a Divine Revelation is not to be rigidly demonstrated. It exists only for faith,—only for him to whom it proves itself by begetting faith in him."

and supernatural enlightenment. The religious faculty natural to man may, by centuries of sustained effort and instructive experience, produce surprising results, but these results may be distinguished from the attainments made by a race under the continuous influence of a special revelation, and from the truths communicated by God's interposition. We are on all hands surrounded by results of the steady application of men's natural faculties so astonishing that we may well be cautious in denying anything to their power. Man has, *e. g.*, a natural capacity for music, and the picture which Lucian gives of Hermes constructing the first lyre out of the shell of a dead tortoise may rather overrate the ingenuity of those who first attempted to express the feeling for music that was in them. If we listen to the tom-toms that stir the painted savage to his war-dance, and then to the most overpowering of Beethoven's symphonies, we apprehend the range of human faculty and the development of which it is susceptible. But, keeping this in view, and bearing in mind also that to establish the fact of a revelation it must be shown that the faculty of the race to which it was given was not competent to attain the idea it accepts, we think this can be made good regarding the idea of the Incarnation of our Lord.

It is the Incarnation, God revealed in human nature, which is the essential formative characteristic of Christianity. It is the Incarnation which is the Revelation to which all other revelation was preliminary and preparatory. But if the science of religion has reached any trustworthy conclusions at all, one of these certainly is that the idea of incarnation is alien to the Semitic mind. The characteristic of the Semitic conception of God is that it sets an impassable gulf between God and man, while the mythologies of the Aryan peoples exhibit a familiar intercourse between heaven and earth. It is often difficult to say who is a god and who is a man, or whether the recognised god has more of the human or of the divine. Let us hear one of our very best authorities on this point.[1] "Neither as monotheisms, nor as polytheisms, do the Semitic religions attribute a fatherly, humane character to their gods. Even the Old Testament knows only an abstract ideal fatherhood, which the Hebrews as a nation realise, but the Hebrew as a man almost never does. The Semitic God dwells in inaccessible light—an awful, invisible presence, before which man must stand uncovered, trembling; but the Indo-European God is pre-eminently accessible,

[1] Fairbairn's *Studies*, p. 36; comp. Dorner's *Person of Christ*, Introd.

loves familiar intercourse, is bound to man by manifold ties of kinship."

If, then, this professed incarnation had occurred upon the ground of an Indo-European religion, it might plausibly have been referred to the natural craving of the Indo-European for such manifestations. The idea is not alien to the mind of that race, and this circumstance would have prejudiced the fact. But occurring, as the incarnation does, among a Semitic people, it is impossible to believe that this idea was a natural growth—the mere result of the unaided working of Semitic instincts. These instincts lay all in an opposite direction. Even the Jews who became Christians showed a strong repugnance and almost incapacity to believe in our Lord's divinity. They fell back into Ebionism and betrayed their Semitic nature. In the mind of Mohammed the idea of an incarnation could find no place. It was with a revulsion of feeling and a passionate indignation, altogether unlike the quiet unconcern of our European Unitarians, that the Arabian prophet denounced as horrible blasphemy the idea that Jesus was God. Here, then, we have the root-idea of a religion springing up from a soil in which there was nothing which could naturally produce it; that is to say, we have an idea which perfectly answers to the definition of a revelation which the science of religion gives us—an idea "given," not acquired. I confess I do not see how to evade the conclusion that this is a genuine revelation.

The case is very much strengthened when we consider that the idea was conveyed by the fact of incarnation. The idea did not first arise in the mind of a religious teacher, neither did it first take possession of a race and subsequently give birth to the fact. It was the fact which gave birth to the idea in the minds of the few who understood it; it was the overpowering evidence of the fact itself which overcame the Semitic repugnance in so far as it was overcome. Men felt that it was not an idea about God they were receiving by revelation, but that God was revealing Himself. It is the fact of the incarnation that is the revelation.

What we have, then, in the Christian religion is this: we have the highest idea of God which has ever actually been conceived by any race or individual; and it may therefore safely be said the highest possible. But this idea has been in point of fact conveyed through the incarnation. The prominent idea, therefore, in the Christian conception of God is that which the incarnation presents; that is, the idea of a God who can and does become incarnate, a God therefore of a moral nature similar to our own, and of a boundless love. But this incarnation, while it proves itself to be a revelation of God by giving us the highest possible conception of God, has also been proved to be a revelation by the soil in which it took root. There seems therefore sufficient ground to affirm that Christianity is not only the best religion, but the only true religion. Its Founder blesses mankind not by His superior moral teaching mainly, nor only by His giving us better information about God than other teachers, but by His bringing God into the world, by showing us our God suffering with and for us, and thus bringing an altogether new thing into the world, a thing in respect of which no other teacher can rival or imitate Him. It is because He and He alone has done this, that the religion thus founded alone deserves the title of the true religion, and stands upon a distinctly different footing from all other religions. There is that in it which essentially distinguishes it from those religions which can be traced to the unaided operation of the religious faculty in man. In Mohammedanism we find no evidence of revelation strictly so called. It is very easy to detect the roots of Mohammedanism in the pre-existing social condition of Arabia, and in the religions to which Mohammed had access. Buddha, again, by the atheistic principle of his religion, repudiated all idea of revelation.[1]

There are other peculiarities of the Christian religion which confirm the impression that it essentially differs from other religions, and is not the mere outgrowth of the natural faculty of a race or of highly gifted individuals. It connects itself with a series of revelations extending in one line through the entire preceding history of the world. The argument in favour of a primitive revelation has, so far as I see, been rather evaded than met. It is quite true that no revelation could create in man the religious faculty; you might as well try to create in man the gills of a fish by throwing him into the water. But does the fact that man was created with a capacity to know God imply that antecedently to any revelation he knew Him? The innate belief in the supernatural, and the accompanying craving for communion with a personal God, implies only such knowledge as the infant has of the language he has a capacity for learning but has yet to learn. This capacity for knowing God implies that unless the true idea of God is presented, man will for himself conceive some idea of the Divine; but it certainly does not

[1] On the claims of later Buddhism to be a revealed religion, see Müller's *Ancient Sanskrit Lit.* pp. 82–6.

imply that without the presentation to him of the true idea he will himself arrive at it. It is quite conceivable that man should have been enabled to make such use of the revelation of God in nature and providence as to prepare him for receiving the personal revelation in the incarnation. Paul, indeed, distinctly affirms that this was possible. But the history of natural religions proves that men have not in point of fact so used their natural advantages. And that idea of God which is recognised as the highest connects itself historically with what professes to be a primitive revelation.

The difficulty that is started by the question, How could this revelation be made? does not seem a very serious one. Why must it have been, as is asserted, either oral or written? Why may it not have been by an impression produced on the mind, or by dream or vision, or by any of those methods to which the human mind in an unsophisticated state has shown itself susceptible? Whatever was the method by which the communication was made, here is the fact, that the earliest tradition known to exist among men contains in it a prediction which authenticates itself by its fulfilment at least 1500 years after its being committed to writing. Where did this prediction—that the seed of the woman would bruise the serpent's head—come from? It is vague, but it has just the same vagueness which every embryo has. The lines are already there on which the definite organism is to be developed, and by these lines the whole future development is already determined.

Again, the development of the idea of God on this line has this distinguishing feature, that it is *historical.* It is not the result of human speculation, however earnest and enlightened, but of impressions made from without, by God Himself, on the history of a people. In the sacred books of other religions we have hymns full of devotional feeling and thoughts about God which surprise us by their truth, but in the Bible we have mainly a history of what God Himself has done in the world to pave the way for His appearing in it. Instead of the fanciful mythological stories which pleased the Greek mind in its childhood, we have a serious, prosaic, ever-progressing, consistent revelation of God in national history. It is the Being who moves the history, and makes Himself felt at every critical time of it, who *by doing so* communicates the knowledge of Himself, His ways, and His purposes. It supplies, that is to say, the very element which constitutes revelation as distinguished from conjecture or research, and unquestionably that very element which has always been lacking in other religions. Dr. Newman has expressed this in his own unrivalled manner. "While Natural Religion was not without provision for all the deepest and truest religious feelings, yet presenting no tangible history of the Deity, no points of His personal character (if we may so speak without irreverence), it wanted that most efficient incentive to all action, a starting or rallying point—an object on which the affections could be placed and the energies concentrated. Common experience in life shows how the most popular and interesting cause languishes if its head be removed; and how political power is often vested in individuals merely for the sake of the definiteness of the practical impression which a personal presence produces."[1] In short, men need to know God not as they learn a doctrine, but as they become acquainted with a person.

It is, I think, in this direction that we find the most valuable light on the connection between Christianity and other religions. The idea of God presented by Christ has in its essential features been very nearly approached by Hindu and Greek speculation. The Christian idea is indeed absent from all the other great religions. These religions have certainly not succeeded in setting before the minds of

[1] *University Sermons*, p. 23.

men such a conception of God as can be justified to a well-informed and religious mind. But under these religions individual speculators have constantly been arising to proclaim the fallacy of the popular conception and to revive the conception of one Supreme and more or less Spiritual Being. And, moreover, there is discernible in various polytheistic religions a background of monotheism and that sense of an Invisible Upholder of all things which seems ineradicable from the human mind. But this vague monotheistic craving, and this high and admirable speculation of thoughtful and earnest men, have come to nothing, and have told far less than they might have been expected to tell on the religions of the world, for lack of the one thing which Christianity has—certainty in its declaration of the God men instinctively crave. In other words, there is recognisable here precisely the distinction we should expect between revelation and speculation or craving. We find that majestic and loving Presence which men of deep religious feeling have always longed for now fixed in a definite form before men's eyes and proclaimed with authority and assurance. We find, therefore, this idea becoming the property, not of a few exceptional men, but of all; becoming the informing spirit of a religion. Had men of profound religious feeling never "felt after" such a God as Christ reveals, we might have doubted whether this were the God most suited to our nature because the God who created it; but had this God never been revealed in Christ we should now have been no further on than were the scholars of Plato or Marcus Aurelius, with occasional passing conceptions of the true God, but longing that we *knew* Him. The relation between revelation and speculation is precisely the relation between Christianity and the best thoughts of men under other religions.

This is not reasoning in a circle. We do not receive the assurance because we first believe this to be a revelation, but the professed revelation is in a form which gives definiteness and assurance. In the person and life of Christ there is brought before men's minds, without effort on their part, the very God who has been felt after by the highest-minded men. We have God in history, God in the world visible to men.

II.—We pass now to the second function which religion performs. Every religion aims not only at giving men a true conception of the supernatural, but also at bringing men into harmony with the supernatural. The best religion will be that which furnishes the highest idea of the supernatural and at the same time brings men most efficiently and perfectly into harmony with it. Now it is manifest that the Christian religion, founded as it is in the Incarnation, exhibits the closest possible harmony between man and that which is beyond nature. It is only at first sight that the union which Brahmanism preaches seems more complete. The absorption of the human soul into the soul of the world involves the extinction of man's personality, and therefore cannot be its fullest development. The union presented by Christianity is the closest possible between two *persons*—an absolute conformity of will. The union between God and man which the Christian religion proclaims is exhibited in the incarnation, and is there shown to be of so perfect a kind that God and man can act as one person. The *summum bonum* held out to man is the highest conceivable—a perfect personal union with God. It is not a mere external Paradise that Christianity presents to our hope, it is not mere deliverance from punishment nor a liberal reward of virtue, but this religion proposes nothing short of that utmost good which man can imagine—such a resemblance in character to the Highest Being as will bring us into the most perfect harmony with Him and consequently with all that His will rules.

This is the union with God which Christianity proposes—a personal union dependent on character; and undoubtedly it is, so far, superior to other religions. But does it actually accomplish what it proposes? The accomplishment of its end involves the highest moral teaching and the strongest moral influence.

We may assume, as pretty generally admitted, that no religion surpasses the Christian in moral teaching. This indeed is involved in the admission that Christianity presents the highest conception of God; because this conception of God is given through a human life, and this human life must therefore present us with the highest conception of human attainment and of human character. The morality of Buddhism may very fairly be compared with Christian morality, but it is unnecessary to enter into any detailed comparison of the ideal Buddhist with the ideal Christian, because Buddhism has notoriously failed to make men moral. And it is not enough that a religion provide healthy moral teaching, it must also furnish us with the most powerful moral energy. It must be able to bring men to the perfect character it depicts. We must compare religions not only in regard to the ideal their founders have conceived, but also in regard to their actual results on races and individuals.

To estimate the value of a religion by its results is always a task of great difficulty, for the influence of a religion never operates in a solitary and separate manner, but always in complication with the influences of government, civilisation, and race. Much has recently been attributed to Islam which is unquestionably due to the native and ineradicable ferocity and barbarism of the Turks. The characteristics of race and even the habits of a heathen ancestry survive and crop up through all the growth of the imported religion. In the very birthplace of Islam, among the Bedouins of the desert, it would be difficult to say whether their customs are more pagan or Mohammedan. They use pagan oaths and call their children by heathenish names; they practise the scarification common among savages in proof of manhood; they decide disputes by the ordeal of licking red-hot iron, and are addicted to other customs too shocking for ears polite.[1] To judge of Islam by such adherents would evidently be as unfair as to judge of Christianity by the licentious and infamous Coptic monks. The Bedouins themselves decline being accepted as fair specimens of the product of Islam, though, like most other people, they ascribe their irreligion to their unfortunate circumstances. "We pray not," they say, "because we must *drink* the water of ablution; we give no alms, because we have to ask them; we fast not the Ramazan month, because we starve throughout the year;

[1] Burton's *Pilgrim.* iii. 79, 80.

and we do no pilgrimage, because the world is the house of Allah."[1]

Again, if we look about for a fair representation of the character formed by the Koran, we are perplexed by the endless varieties of belief and consequently of character embraced in Islam. To which of its seventy-three sects are we to look for the fair average Mohammedan? Is the Persian freethinker, who dares to find contradictions in the Koran and to wish there were no Friday in the week,[2] the fit specimen, or shall we rather look to the fanatical Wahabi, who adds smoking as well as drinking to the catalogue of deadly sins? Shall we inspect the habits of the Hayetis and Hadathites, who ascribe divinity to Jesus, or those of the quietist Sufis, of whom the orthodox Moslem holds such an opinion that he thinks it more meritorious to kill a Sufi than to save ten human lives? Were we to accept the first Khalifs and their followers as the normal type of Mohammedan character, we should say that a manly contempt for the luxuries and pomps of life, an unrivalled enthusiasm for the propagation of Islam, prompt and untiring energy, unostentatious piety, fearlessness and disinterested loyalty, were its most striking features.

[1] Burton's *Pilgrim.*; and cf. Burckhardt's *Notes*, i. 379.

[2] Gobineau, *Les Religions*, p. 118.

But some of these elements are sadly lacking in the degenerate days of secure prosperity and well-established empire.

Again, in estimating the results of a religion, allowance must be made for the influence of individual temperament. We would as little accept the blood-thirsty Khaled as the noble Hosein as a fair representative of the influence of Islam. It is related of Hosein that a slave, having accidentally thrown over him the contents of a scalding dish while he sat at dinner, fell on his knees and repeated the verse of the Koran, "Paradise is for those who bridle their anger." "I am not angry," said Hosein. The slave proceeded, "And for those who forgive men." "I forgive you," answered Hosein. Whereupon the slave audaciously finished the verse, "God loveth the beneficent." "I give you your liberty and 400 pieces of silver," replied the faithful Moslem.

Such are some of the cautions to be observed in an inquiry into the results of any religion. It must be borne in mind that in order to have a deep impression, the seal must not only be deeply cut, there must also be a sufficient depth of wax to receive its impress. No doubt Christianity shows better than some other religions because it has been accepted by superior races. It has not the whole credit of European civilisation; but, on the other hand, it has fairly the credit of approving itself to these superior races, and, to say the very least, of allying itself with every beneficent agency. That language is the best which adapts itself most readily to every advance in science and philosophy, and most perfectly covers all the requirements of a rapidly developing social state; and that religion is the best which, even if it be not considered the root of all that is acceptable among the most civilised races, does at least keep pace with the most fully and rapidly developing civilisation.

It is of course out of the question to attempt here any detailed comparison of the moral condition of Christian and other countries. The superiority of Christianity may be more summarily established. The only religion which can reasonably be compared with Christianity in point of moral influence is Mohammedanism. The teaching of Buddhism is much purer and more elevated, but it has failed to make its adherents moral. Mohammedanism, while promulgating a much less lofty code, has succeeded to a very considerable extent in enforcing that code. In the words of Dean Stanley: "Within a confined circle the code of the Koran makes doubtless a deeper impression than has been made on Christians by the code of the Bible."[1]

[1] *Eastern Church*, p. 279.

But the means by which Mohammedanism effects this is not the most perfect moral agency. It is, like police regulations, effective within a certain circumference, but leaving a large margin beyond; and, like every external law, it proposes to form the character through the conduct, and not the conduct through the character. The Koran tells men their duty and enforces its precepts by the promise of rewards and by the threat of punishment. It provides no higher impulse to conduct than a sense of duty may inspire. Now, a sense of duty is an influence with which no man can dispense; but it is not the most effective moral force, neither can it alone bring human character to a perfect development. Man has not attained resemblance to his ideal, to his God, if he still needs any external constraint to compel him to duty, and has not that love of what is right which alone raises God Himself above all outward law. There is something lacking in our resemblance to God until we not merely do what He commands, and recognise as right what He delights in, but ourselves are possessed by a spontaneous delight in all that is right, and do it because, like God, we love it. That religion which makes no provision for transforming ourselves as well as our conduct, that religion which cannot make us like God by furnishing us with a genuine relish for all that is holy, is not the best, the ultimate religion. But if there be a religion which offers us the very spirit of God, which recognises that law does not bring life with it, and which, therefore, makes provision not only for our instruction but also for communicating to us an inward and spontaneous and permanent relish for all that we ought to do, this can alone claim to be the ultimate religion. Happiness is a word and no more to us until religion accomplish this for us. Now this is the rational and perfectly satisfying prospect which Christianity affords, and in proof that it is not a dream, the Founder of the religion exemplifies in His own veritable life upon earth that the attainment of perfect conformity with God is possible to human nature, and He offers to all His disciples the very spirit which made Him what He was—the same source of inward life which was always sufficient for Himself.

We are now in a position to say how much truth there is in the assertion so frequently made, that the difference between religions is a difference of degree and not of kind. If by this it be meant that all religions satisfy in a greater or less degree the religious cravings of men, the assertion is a very harmless, and, at the same time, very obvious one. All food might in the same way be said to be of one kind, because even the human flesh, which would fill a European with disgust, satisfies the appetite of the cannibal. All language may on the same principle be said to be of one kind, because even the birdlike chirping of the aborigines of Malacca expresses their desires and wants, perhaps better than Greek or English could. But a classification so wide becomes useless. The difference between Aryan and Semitic languages is not a difference of degree but of kind. A language of the one kind can by no process be improved into a language of the other kind. You might as well try to improve a camel into a dray-horse. Both are beasts of burden, but the difference between them is not a difference in degree. The one cannot be improved into the other. And it seems to tend rather to confusion than to clearness of thought to assert that religions differ only in degree, and that there is no essential difference between a natural and a revealed religion. What should be affirmed is that the religious faculty in men differs only in degree; that the man who at present is a polytheist may have this faculty so developed as to become a monotheist; as a negro who has grown up speaking his own barbarous tongue, will, if educated, prefer and need Arabic or English. But the negro dialect does not develope into the higher language, neither does the lower religion develope into the higher. The one must be laid aside that the other may be assumed, as the Red Indian must doff his feathers and buffalo robe before he puts on the dress of a higher civilisation.

It need scarcely be added that, notwithstanding this essential distinction among religions, scientific investigation must, as far as possible, discard all prepossession in favour of any particular religion, and must especially avoid any classification of religions which prejudges the whole question of the relation which religions hold to one another. We cannot start on any such investigation by classifying religions into true and false, natural and revealed, or any divisions which may not be warranted by the results of the investigation. A scientific inquiry, however, may very well conclude with such a classification. And, I may add, that there is nothing absurd in even antecedently expecting that religions may fall into two great classes of natural and revealed, because in religion we have these two great factors to deal with—the natural faculty in man and its confessedly supernatural object. And it is not an unlikely thing that, according as the one or the other of these factors predominates, an essentially distinct religion may be produced. The racial or ethnological classification of religions is convenient and significant; and, had we to deal with a purely natural product, such as language or art, it might be not only serviceable but sufficient. In religion, however, we have to deal with a supernatural element, and a racial classification seems to me to leave no room for a factor which *may* be found more influential in differentiating or producing new religions than even race distinctions.

III. — Having determined the comparative intrinsic value of Christianity and other religions, two important questions remain to be answered. Have these inferior religions answered the purposes of religion? and, Have they in any case answered these purposes better than Christianity itself would have done?

To the first of these questions every one will, I presume, answer in a general affirmative, while in regard to the *degree* in which the purposes of religion have been accomplished by the various faiths of the world, a considerable variety of opinion will be found to prevail. If the purpose of religion is to bring men into harmony with God, it must be acknowledged that some of the religions of the world have not done much towards the accomplishment of this end. They have maintained in men's minds a false conception of God, and have misdirected the natural yearnings of men to attain a lasting harmony with Him. But there is one important purpose which all religions have served—they have kept the religious faculty alive from one generation to another. The efforts this religious faculty has made to satisfy itself have been often like the vain wavings and ineffectual graspings instinctively made by the tentacles of some marine creature to anchor itself in a storm, efforts which, however ineffectual, do yet keep alive the instincts which guide them and betray the normal habits of the animal. So every movement and utterance of the religious faculty in man has served at least to keep it alive, and hereby at once to evince and to maintain, if not to develope, his capacity for the highest religion. This is the first purpose which is served by every religion.

Other purposes also are served. Some of these are well presented by Professor Max Müller in the following passage. "An old Samoyede woman who was asked by Castrèn whether she ever said her prayers, replied: 'Every morning I step out of my tent and bow before the sun, and say, "When thou risest, I, too, rise from my bed." And every evening I say, "When thou sinkest down, I, too, sink down to rest."' That was her prayer, perhaps the whole of her religious service; a poor prayer it may seem to us, but not to her, for it made that old woman look twice at least every day away from earth and up to heaven; it implied that her life was bound up with a larger and higher life; it encircled the daily routine of her earthly existence with something of a Divine halo. She herself was evidently proud of it, for she added, with a touch of self-righteousness, 'There *are* wild people who never say their morning and evening prayers.'"[1] It is easy, no doubt, to go too far in the direction of spiritualizing rude superstitions and formal observances, but a religious mind will always import its own sentiment into the forms it has access to; and it is to be considered that the best of religions, in common with the lowest, are for the religious and not for the irreligious. And, as in the instance of this old woman, so in countless others it will be found that religions of a somewhat low type have exercised an elevating and comforting influence on their sincere adherent. To pray daily, even to a deaf and unconscious god, is certainly to acknowledge dependence on, and a hopeful connection with, a higher and intelligent power. Apart altogether from the question whether such misdirected prayer does not move the compassion of the living God, it certainly introduces into the life of the worshipper an influence which must be, in however limited a degree, elevating

[1] Max Müller's *Introd.* p. 201.

and counteractive of selfish and sensual motives. In the well-chosen words of Professor Jowett, "The first step has been made from sense and appetite into the ideal world. He who denies himself something, who offers up a prayer, who practises a penance, performs an act, not of necessity, nor of choice, but of duty; he does not simply follow the dictates of passion, though he may not be able to give a reason for the performance of his act. He whose God comes first in his mind has an element within him which in a certain degree sanctifies his life by raising him above himself. He has some common interest with other men, some unity in which he is comprehended with them. There is a preparation for thoughts yet higher."[1]

That which compels us to make large allowance for religions which seem to have little in them that is either true or impressive, is the circumstance that they have in all ages and countries proved themselves capable of nourishing men of remarkable religious insight and fervour. It is a familiar fact that a deeply religious spirit may find more nutriment and stimulus in a religion of a somewhat low type than a man of feeble religious faculty will find even in the highest religion. The history of Hinduism brings before us many instances in point. Here, *e.g.*, are some

[1] Jowett's *Epistles of Paul*, ii. 465.

of the devout utterances of Dadu, a religious reformer who lived about the year 1600.

"Dadu sayeth: Thou, O God! art the author of all things which have been made, and from Thee will originate all things which are to be made. Thou art the Maker and the Cause of all things made. There is none other but Thee.

"He is my God, who maketh all things perfect. Meditate upon Him in whose hands are life and death.

"I believe that God made man, and that He maketh everything. He is my friend.

"Let faith in God characterise all your thoughts, words, and actions. He who serveth God placeth confidence in nothing else.

"If He that perfecteth mankind occupy a place in your hearts, you will experience His happiness inwardly. Ram is in everything, Ram is eternal.

"In order that He may diffuse happiness, God becometh subservient to all; and although the knowledge of this is in the hearts of the foolish, yet will they not praise His name.

"Dadu sayeth: I will become the sacrifice of the Godhead; do unto me, O God, as Thou thinkest best. I am obedient to Thee. My disciples! behold no other God. Fix your heart on God and be humble as though you were dead. He that partaketh of but one grain of the love of God shall be released from the sinfulness of all his doubts and actions." [1]

It is, however, only one part of the truth which is expressed by a very eminent authority, when he says: "However imperfect, however childish a religion may be, it always places the human soul in the presence of God; and however imperfect and however childish the conception of God may be, it always represents the highest ideal of perfection which the human soul, for the time being, can reach and grasp. Religion therefore places the human soul in the presence of its highest ideal, it lifts it above the level of ordinary goodness, and produces at least a yearning after a higher and better life—a life in the light of God." [2] This statement must be corrected by the remembrance that there have been religions in the world which did not place the human soul in the presence of its highest ideal—religions which prevailed for many centuries and among nations otherwise enlightened, and which represented the Divine as more licentious and treacherous than the human. Zeus and Hermes represented the ideal of a barbarous age, and these representa-

[1] Wilson's *Works*, i. 106–109.

[2] Max Müller's *Introd.* p. 263.

tions, receiving the prestige of worship, cramped the national thought and morality, and instead of nourishing the roots of all helpful social and political agencies, unceasingly retarded and counteracted them. In fact, as a still more trustworthy authority informs us, "they changed the truth of God into a lie." They were *false* religions; as false as the geographies or the cosmogonies of the same origin; true only in so far as the religious faculty in man declares for a supernatural of some kind. In short, there is no stronger argument for the necessity of a revelation than the history of natural religions. Whatever may be said of individuals, it must be acknowledged that the great religions of the world present most misleading conceptions of God and of the way to become one with Him.[1]

But while we condemn many religious systems as exhibiting more of error than of truth, we must beware of pronouncing judgment on the individuals who by means of these systems, or in spite of these systems, have endeavoured to find God and to live the highest and purest life conceivable by them. It is my belief that no man is savingly united to God without the aid of Christ's Spirit. At the same time I believe that God's care and compassion extend not only to those to whom His

[1] See Jowett's strongly condemnatory criticism of the Greek religion in the paper above cited.

extraordinary revelations have penetrated, but to all men under whatever religion they are now living; and if we are at all to judge who have the Spirit of Christ, we must judge not by men's possession or lack of a knowledge which has been impossible to them, but by their conduct. Christ has been made known to us that we may become like Him: if others are liker Him than we are, although they have never heard the name of Jesus, they will enter the kingdom of God before us. Salvation is resemblance to Christ;[1] it is the possession of the Spirit of Christ, and if the fruits of that Spirit are found in the life of those who have known nothing of the historical Christ, we should welcome the idea thus suggested, that apart from this knowledge our Lord may have found means of communicating His Spirit to some.[2]

IV.—But is it not possible, after all, that these religions may have actually been more suitable and more beneficial than Christianity

1 This resemblance, however, must extend not only to the moral character, but also to the attitude towards God maintained by Christ.

2 The truth I am trying to present was never better formulated than in the words of the wise and liberal authors of the Westminster Confession: "All other elect persons [besides infants], who are incapable of being outwardly called by the ministry of the word, are regenerated and saved by Christ through the Spirit, who worketh when, and where, and how He pleaseth."

could have been to the races which adopted them?

"Speaking generally," says Herbert Spencer, "the religion current in each age and among each people has been as near an approximation to the truth as it was then and there possible for men to receive."[1] Similarly we find Max Müller asserting that "in one sense every religion was a true religion, being the only religion which was possible at the time, which was compatible with the language, the thoughts, and the sentiments of each generation, which was appropriate to the age of the world."[2] This opinion has been held by men of various creeds. The Brahman says, "Men of an enlightened understanding well know that the Supreme has imparted to each nation the doctrine most suitable for it, and He therefore beholds with satisfaction the various ways in which He is worshipped."[3] The complacent Chinaman re-echoes the same idea when he replies to the zealous missionary, "Our Josh, your Josh; your Josh for you, our Josh for us; all very good Josh." Mohammed himself seems at times to have entertained a somewhat similar view at least of the Jewish and Christian reli-

[1] *First Principles*, p. 116.

[2] *Introd. to Sc. of Relig.* p. 261.

[3] Hardwick's *Christ and other Masters*, i. 27 (2nd ed.).

gions. "Unto every one of you have we given a law and an open path; and, if God had pleased, He had surely made you one people; but He hath thought fit to give you different laws, that He might try you in that which He hath given you respectively. Therefore, strive to excel each other in good works: unto God shall ye all return, and then will He declare unto you that concerning which ye have disagreed."[1]

Now, although it is easy to give to such utterances the accent of indifferentism, and to condemn them offhand as putting all religions on a level, there is no doubt that the theory they suggest is worthy of the most patient consideration. The theory that the religion which is absolutely the best is not therefore relatively the best, but is found unsuitable and even inapplicable to certain races in a certain stage of their development, is a theory which claims to base itself in the soundest philosophy of history, and which brings illustrations of its truth from the actual successes and failures of various creeds. When Solon was asked if he had promulgated among the Athenians the best laws, he replied, "The best they are capable of receiving." And so a religion not absolutely the best may be the best which a given nation is capable of receiving.

[1] Sura v. (Sale's Translation).

The great lesson in comparative religion which we learn from the connection of Judaism and Christianity, is that men are not always ripe for the highest religion; that there is a fulness of time which it may take four thousand years to produce. The Mosaic religion, imperfect as it was compared with Christianity, was better for Israel during its period of tutelage and preparation than the religion of Christ would have been. And the question is, How far does this principle apply to the religions which are not the historical forerunners of Christianity? Though Christianity as a historical fact was prepared for by Mosaism alone, may its acceptance as the ultimate religion not be prepared for by any one of the great religions? May not these religions as well as Mosaism serve in their measures as pedagogues, keeping the nations from running away from all religious teaching? Have they not kept alive in men the thirst for God and some faint knowledge of His accessibility and oversight of the world?

In answer to these questions, it is obvious to remark, in the first place, that Mosaism, being itself a revealed religion, stands on so different a footing from natural religions that we cannot argue from it to them. There is evidence that it was designed as a preparation for Christianity; the providential design of the other religions is as yet unascertained, and they can be considered preparations for Christianity only in the limited sense of keeping before men's minds some idea of God and of religious duty. Experience indeed seems to show that practically they are in many cases hindrances to the acceptance of any better religion.

And it is to be remarked, secondly, that the above-cited assertion of Mr. Spencer is purely gratuitous and incapable of verification. Apart from experiment, it cannot be ascertained what religion any age or people is capable of receiving. Christianity has been accepted by the most unpromising races; and, for all Mr. Spencer knows, had it been offered, it might long ago have been accepted by tribes that have lived for centuries, and are still living, under such "approximation to the truth" as devil-worship or Sivaism affords.

But the primitive history of Mohammedanism in Arabia is sometimes cited as an instance in which it seems that where Christianity could effect little or nothing for a people, an inferior religion effected much. And although Mohammedanism is no fair specimen of natural religion, having so largely borrowed from Judaism, yet it is worth while to look at the facts, and estimate exactly the amount of truth there is in the assertion. It is not denied that this religion did at once effect reforms which Christianity had failed to effect; it accomplished more for Arabia in a few years than Christianity had accomplished in centuries. It abolished at a stroke the idolatry against which Christianity had fought in vain, and it introduced an idea of God which, though imperfect, was at least similar to, as it was borrowed from, the Jewish idea. And to this day Mohammedanism has a greater influence on the outward conduct of the masses than Christianity has. And Mohammedanism has this greater influence precisely because it is an inferior religion, trusting more to law than to the spirit. The command to abstain from wine is no more emphatic than the Christian command to avoid drunkenness, but it is imbedded in a religion of precept, rule, and outward authority; whereas Christians are left more to their individual feeling and conscience, and are encouraged to become a law to themselves. Mohammedans are treated as children, and behave themselves as boys in school. Christians are treated as men, and often show that they are not worthy of such treatment.

It is therefore idle to imagine that if Mohammed had become a Christian, and had preached the religion of Christ with the same zeal and determination which characterised his preaching of Islam, the result would have been an extension of Christianity as wide and enduring and fruitful as the extension of Mohammedanism has proved. It is idle to make any such supposition as this, because had Mohammed been a Christian he could not have used the instruments he did use, either for the extension of his religion among surrounding nations, or for the enforcement of its precepts upon those who accepted it. It is not the seeming accident that the one religion enjoyed the services of an apostle more zealous and skilful than any enjoyed by the rival creed; it is not this which gave success to Islam where Christianity had failed, but that the more spiritual creed by its very spirituality precluded the use of such instruments of propagation and enforcement as the inferior creed could use. The comparative failure of Christianity in Arabia and in the neighbouring countries where Islam enjoyed its most signal triumphs is not accounted for by that which is accidental, but only by that which is essential to the one religion and to the other. Christianity failed, in so far as it did fail, because its nature required it to attempt to "guide by the eye" men whose dispositions and habits could be governed only by the more palpable and inviolable restraints of bit and bridle. It failed because the Arabs did not desire to be "righteous overmuch," but desiderated a religion which gave them liberal allowances both in this world and the next. They took to Mohammedanism because it solved the problem and showed them how they could please God by pleasing themselves. They enlarged their inheritance in heaven by conquering a broader heritage on earth, and took the kingdom of heaven by pillage and slaughter. The purer the form, therefore, in which Christianity had been presented to the Arabians, the less likely was it that they would accept it.

It is, however, pertinent to inquire whether the rapid acceptance of Islam and the consequent improvement in morality was worth the price paid for it. The triumph of Islam was the doom of the highest form of religion. No doubt it was not very probable that Christianity would either be intelligently accepted in Arabia or would become in a pure form the sole religion of the countries now Mohammedan; but the triumph of Islam turned this improbability into an impossibility. These countries are less open to Christianity than those more barbarous lands in which religions much more unlike our own have prevailed. In point of fact Islam has not educated its adherents to the reception of a more spiritual religion than itself. Spiritual men it has reared: under all religions there arise men whose spiritual desires burst the bonds of the system that first helped them to understand things divine. But the nations which have accepted Islam cannot be said to be any nearer accepting Christianity now, or any better prepared for the highest form of religion than the Arabs to whom Mohammed preached. Now, an illustration of the nature of the evil thus wrought in the world lies to our hand. Most of our statesmen and leaders of opinion vehemently object to anything like paternal government or the infringement of the liberty of the subject. They do not question that a strong hand might put down some of our national vices, and make us show better on statistical tables of morality. An entire repression of the liquor traffic and a relentless punishment of offenders would go far to remove one stain from the face of society. Why then is this not done? Because it is believed that the gain would be more apparent than real, and that it would not compensate for the loss of individual liberty. That is to say, it is recognised that nothing is so precious as self-government, and that enforced virtue is apt to develope into some more hideous and deep-seated vice. They recognise that a country may really be in a healthier and far more hopeful state when liberty is turned into license than when outward respectability is secured by ignominious despotism.

But the gain which Mohammedanism brought was of a kind analogous to that which is secured by outward authority: it secured immediate reformation at the price of future growth.

The conclusion then which, it seems to me, is fairly deducible from these facts, is this, that there are conditions of society, as there are states and stages of the individual character, to which Christianity appeals in vain,[1] or in which, if it does succeed in finding a nominal acceptance, it remains inoperative. And undoubtedly in such a case it is better that there be an inferior religion accepted than none at all, supposing always that this inferior religion be one which is not wholly false and evil. But if this inferior religion be one which by its nature is unsusceptible of progress, and still more if it turns the present incapacity to accept Christianity into a formal opposition to it, it may

[1] These states are not always charactererised by a backward civilization, or by a low *physique*. What does characterise them, is a question too vast to discuss here. Christian missions have succeeded among the most degraded races, while among nations in more favourable conditions their success has been tardy and doubtful. Our Scotch missions in India are wisely worked on the understanding that no great immediate success is to be looked for, but that every agency which indoctrinates the community with a healthy morality in business, or with a respect for law, or with the Christian ideas of excellence in any department of human life, necessarily aids in securing the ultimate triumph of Christianity.

reasonably be questioned whether the permanent disability it entails does not far outweigh the immediate benefit it confers. In other words, we conclude that what is true in every other department of human life is true also of religion. The Red Indian, who receives most important information from a few rude figures carved on the bark of a tree, can make no use whatever of a written description of the country. A despotism is not the absolutely best form of government, but it is undeniably the best for nations at a certain stage of political development. But the benefit of its adoption by any people will be shown especially in the success with which it trains them to acknowledge and adopt some higher and more perfect form of government. A milk diet is very poor food for the adult, but it is the only food which an infant can receive or find any nourishment in. Its suitableness for the infant, however, may be measured precisely by its success in fitting him to long for and utilize the food of the adult. The government of one race by another, as in our Indian Empire, is not an ideal political condition, but probably a large proportion of the subject race would acknowledge that self-government had become impossible to them, or, at all events, that their subjection brings them advantages superior to any they could otherwise have attained. If, however, these advantages do not fit them for self-government, if familiarity with our customs, laws, literature, government, and history, does not lift them above the condition in which we found them, and make them capable of the highest forms of national life, it may be questioned, and it will be doubted, whether, after all, their present condition of subjection has been even relatively the best. In like manner it may be granted that Islam was more akin to the Arabs of the seventh century than Christianity, and did good which Christianity had not done, but it is the reproach of Islam that it has not trained its adherents to the reception of Christianity.[1]

It may still be asked, What is the practical outcome of these facts and principles? what is their bearing on missionary effort? If there are tribes so rude that they cannot conceive of God at all without a visible symbol of His presence; if there are races so savage that they must pass through the discipline of a legal religion before they can be trusted with a re-

[1] It is awkward to omit what is really an essential element of this argument—the discussion of the question whether there are any races strictly non-progressive; but space is denied me, and I can only say that, while it seems as if some nations, like some families, had already exhausted their chances and must now die out, it cannot be said that any which survive are incapable of progress.

ligion that is wholly inward; if there is no department of human affairs in which we need more carefully to distinguish between what is absolutely and what is relatively the best—may not a missionary err in preaching the gospel to every creature, and might he not be better employed in preaching some religion which the people would accept? Now, in the first place, missionaries do in fact recognise some individuals and races as hopeful, others as hopeless; and in doing so they follow the example of their Master. Again, it is obvious that the only infallible way to detect who are capable of accepting Christianity is to offer it to all. He would be a very presumptuous man who should, previous to experiment, take upon him to say of any nation or race that it was impervious to Christian truth. Neither can any one predict at what stage or period or turn of affairs any country will at length yield to a persistent and wise, though hitherto ineffectual attempt to Christianize it. The religion of Christ is fitted to become the universal religion, although it is impossible to foresee what agencies may be requisite to bring all nations to the point of accepting it. And while we may be glad that in the absence of Christianity men have derived some comfort, hope, and stimulus from inferior religions, every one who appreciates the work of Christ will do what he can that as rapidly as possible He may be acknowledged by all men as "the way, the truth, and the life." Besides, in the midst of nations which as a whole lack the moral tone that predisposes to the reception of the most spiritual religion, there may be exceptional individuals far surpassing the general national character. It was so to some extent with the Jews. As a whole they proved themselves unable to accept the religion of Christ, and yet among them were found exceptional men who so appreciated and received the religion, that on them the Church was built. Above all, the man whose own convictions of the truth are profound will utter himself in the face of all discouraging appearances. To quote the words of one whose own experience of the receptiveness of his generation has been somewhat mixed: "The highest truth the wise man sees he will fearlessly utter; knowing that, let what may come of it, he is thus playing his right part in the world—knowing that if he can effect the change he aims at—well: if not—well also; though not *so* well."[1]

[1] Herbert Spencer's *First Principles*, p. 123.

Works by the same Author.

I.

THE PARABLES OF OUR LORD. Second Series. The Parables Recorded by St. Luke. Third Thousand. Crown 8vo, cloth, 3*s.* 6*d.*

"Dr. Dods, has no less in this volume than in that in which he illustrated the parables as recorded by St. Matthew, given his readers expositions of marvellous clearness and insight. Everywhere he is simple, direct, and lucid, but always flowing and elevated. His English is strong and idiomatic, and his descriptions and illustrations picturesque and graphic. We heartily commend Dr. Dod's book. Fresh, strong, natural, earnest, it is a credit to Scotch theology, and will be wholesome reading to all honest Christians who peruse it."—*Glasgow Herald.*

II.

THE PARABLES OF OUR LORD. (As Recorded by St. Matthew.) Fourth Thousand. 3*s.* 6*d.*

"There is certainly no better volume on the subject in our language."—*Glasgow Mail.*

"Unfolded with a lucidity which ought to satisfy even Mr. Matthew Arnold. The crisp, pointed, and graphic style of Dr. Dods is in harmony with the keen spiritual insight which marks him out as a prince among the living expositors of the sacred writings."—*Christian Leader.*

III.

THE PRAYER THAT TEACHES TO PRAY. Fifth Edition. Crown 8vo, 2*s.* 6*d.*

"A warm welcome will be given by many to this little book. It is a book to be read in the closet, and from the perusal of which no one can rise without a quickened spiritual life. Unquestionably it will add to the author's reputation."—*Literary World.*

"It is highly instructive, singularly lucid, and unmistakably for quiet personal use."—*Clergyman's Magazine.*

LONDON: HODDER AND STOUGHTON, 27, PATERNOSTER ROW.

Works by the same Author.

IV.

ISAAC, JACOB, AND JOSEPH. Fifth Thousand. 3*s*. 6*d*

"The present volume is worthy of the writer's reputation. He deals with the problems of human life and character, which these biographies suggest, in a candid and manly fashion, and where he discovers a spiritual significance in them, his course is always marked by sobriety and caution, yet he is not wanting in fervour and earnestness."—*Spectator.*

"An admirable example of what biblical exposition for the household ought to be. The freshness and spiritual power of this fresh and strong book are largely due to the author's gift of bringing out the essential characteristics."—*English Presbyterian Messenger.*

V.

ISRAEL'S IRON AGE: Sketches from the Period of the Judges. Fourth Edition. Crown 8vo, cloth, 5*s*.

"Rich in lessons for the daily life, both exterior and interior; lessons which are drawn with much ease from the ancient story, and given in pure, quiet, admirable English."—*British and Foreign Evangelical Review.*

"The popularity of this volume is richly deserved. The sketches are bright and forcible, and abound in moral teaching and practical lessons for the golden age of Victoria as well as for the iron age of Israel."—*Evangelical Magazine.*

"A very thoughtful and instructive contribution to exegetical theology."—*Scotsman.*

"Powerful lectures. This is a noble volume, full of strength. Young men especially will find in it a rich storehouse of prevailing incentive to a godly life. Dr. Dods searches with a masterly hand."—*Nonconformist.*

LONDON: HODDER AND STOUGHTON, 27, PATERNOSTER ROW.

THE PARABLES OF OUR SAVIOUR EXPANDED AND ILLUSTRATED. By W. M. Taylor, D.D., LL.D. 8vo, cloth, 7*s*. 6*d*.

The recent works of Professor Bruce and Siegfried Goebel have broken new ground in this department, and the author's aim has been to turn their fruitful suggestions to good homiletical account. The little volumes of Dr. Dods are full of richest nuggets. But the present work, while indebted in different respects to these authors, will be found to be in others independent of them all. It is published at the urgent request of many who heard the discourses when delivered.

THE LIMITATIONS OF LIFE & OTHER SERMONS. By the same Author. Second Edition. Crown 8vo, cloth, 7*s*. 6*d*.

"Dr. Taylor's Sermons are full of spiritual earnestness and power. They deal with the complex life of men in great cities with much of penetrating wisdom, large sympathy, and tender fidelity."—*London Quarterly Review*.

CONTRARY WINDS AND OTHER SERMONS. By the same Author. Crown 8vo, 7*s*. 6*d*.

"This remarkably able volume of sermons. Dr. Taylor is a master of pulpit oratory, and makes old Evangelical truth glisten afresh in these sermons. His latest book is his best."—*Liverpool Mercury*.

JOHN KNOX. By the same Author. Price 2*s*. 6*d*.

"A short biography, which has two great merits—it presents in short compass, and yet in their true proportions, all the important events of the Reformer's life; and the warm appreciation of Knox's character and achievements by which it is pervaded is never allowed to descend to the level of mere undiscriminating eulogy."—*Scotsman*.

CHRIST AND THE JEWISH LAW. By the Rev. R. Mackintosh, B.D., formerly Cunningham Scholar, New College, Edinburgh. Crown 8vo, 6*s*.

"One of the most remarkable contributions to theological literature that we have received for many years; from a young Scottish scholar."—*Glasgow Mail*.

"Mr. Mackintosh has sought in this volume to exhibit how Christ fulfilled His avowed purpose, not to destroy, but 'to fulfil the Law and the Prophets,' to indicate the manner in which He realized the ethical and ceremonial teaching of the old institution, and in what measure He emancipated both Himself and the future from the dispensation of the past. This has been done by the writer with some skill, insight, and good sense, and in many ways he seems to have taken a just view of the action Christ adopted in connection with the religion of His people."—*Scotsman*.

London: HODDER AND STOUGHTON, 27, Paternoster Row.

The Household Library.

THE PARABLES OF OUR LORD. (The Parables Recorded by St. Matthew). By MARCUS DODS, D.D. Fourth Thousand. Crown 8vo, cloth, 3*s*. 6*d*.

"There is certainly no better volume on the subject in our language."—*Glasgow Mail.*

THE PARABLES OF OUR LORD. Second Series. (The Parables Recorded by St. Luke). By MARCUS DODS, D.D. Third Thousand. Crown 8vo, cloth, 3*s*. 6*d*.

ISAAC, JACOB, AND JOSEPH. By MARCUS DODS, D.D. Fifth Thousand. Crown 8vo, cloth, 3*s*. 6*d*.

"The present volume is worthy of the writer's reputation. He deals with the problems of human life and character which these biographies suggest in a candid and manly fashion, and when he discovers a spiritual significance in them, his course is always marked by sobriety and caution, yet he is not wanting in fervour and earnestness."—*Spectator*.

THE GALILEAN GOSPEL. By Professor A. B. BRUCE, D.D. Second Edition. Crown 8vo, cloth, 3*s*. 6*d*.

"The product of a rich imaginative mind, marked by scholarly analysis, subtle insight, and the suggestiveness of an original and unconventional thinker."—*Glasgow Herald.*

"We heartily commend this little volume as giving an outline ably drawn of the teaching of Christ."—*Spectator*.

THE LORD'S PRAYER. By CHARLES STANFORD, D.D. Second Thousand, Crown 8vo, cloth, 3*s*. 6*d*.

"For spiritual grasp and insight, for wealth of glowing imagery, and for rare felicity of style, it will hold a first place in this valuable series of expository monograms."—*Christian.*

"Beautiful throughout, and cannot fail to be a source of spiritual delight to all who read it."—*British Messenger.*

THE TEMPTATION OF CHRIST. By G S. BARRETT, B.A. Crown 8vo, cloth, 3*s*. 6*d*.

"Intelligent, reverent, and spiritual, marked by much literary beauty."—*British Quarterly Review.*

"Marked alike by careful language and sober thought."—*Guardian.*

THE LAW OF THE TEN WORDS. By J. OSWALD DYKES, D.D., Author of "The Beatitudes," "From Jerusalem to Antioch." Crown 8vo, cloth, 3*s*. 6*d*.

"A delightful series, both cheap and good."—*C, H. Spurgeon.*

"A handy series of admirably printed and very useful volumes."—*Scottish Review.*

LONDON: HODDER AND STOUGHTON, 27, PATERNOSTER ROW.

The Household Library—*Continued.*

THE LIFE OF DAVID, AS REFLECTED IN HIS PSALMS. By ALEXANDER MACLAREN, D.D., of Manchester. Sixth Edition. Crown 8vo., cloth, 3*s.* 6*d.*

"Real gems of exposition are found in this slight work, which might be sought in vain from more erudite and ponderous tomes. . . . We have nothing but admiration and praise for this valuable little reprint."—*Rev. S. Cox, in "Expositor."*

"Just the book we should give to awaken a living and historical interest in the Psalms."—*Guardian.*

THE LAST SUPPER OF OUR LORD, AND HIS WORDS OF CONSOLATION TO THE DISCIPLES. By J. MARSHALL LANG, D.D., Barony Church, Glasgow. Second Edition. Crown 8vo, cloth, 3*s.* 6*d.*

"With a rare power of insight—the result doubtless of much inward experience—Dr. Lang has entered into the very inmost spirit of the scenes and incidents, the words and feelings which make up the history of that night. Earnestness without a tinge of fanaticism is the chief characteristic of the work. Alike in spirit, in tone, and in literary form, this small volume is well fitted to be the devout Christian's companion."—*Scotsman.*

THE SPEECHES OF THE HOLY APOSTLES. By DONALD FRASER, D.D. Second Edition. Crown 8vo, cloth, 3*s.* 6*d.*

"Exceedingly well done."—*Scottish Review.*

"No ephemeral production, but a vigorous presentment of the scope and purpose of the Apostolic Speeches reproducing the facts of the narrative of the Acts of the Apostles in a manner that will serve to make more clear than ever to Bible students what was the actual condition of the early Church."—*Christian.*

ADAM, NOAH, AND ABRAHAM. Readings in the Book of Genesis. By JOSEPH PARKER, D.D., of the City Temple. Third Thousand. Crown 8vo., cloth, 3*s.*

"Sketches of life and character strikingly drawn by a vigorous hand."—*C. H. Spurgeon.*

"An admirable little work, and fully sustains the well-earned reputation of its author as one of the most powerful and practical preachers of the present day."—*Daily Review.*

THE LAMB OF GOD. Expositions in the Writings of St. John. By the Rev. W. R. NICOLL, M.A. Second Edition. Crown 8vo., cloth, 2*s.* 6*d.*

"Replete with the richest thought and finest feeling. The style of the book, too, is as beautiful as the thought and feeling of it, so that it is a feast to read it."—*Aberdeen Free Press.*